THE WAY OF THE SECRET TEMPLE

THE WAY OF THE SECRET TEMPLE
A Third Manual of Occult Training

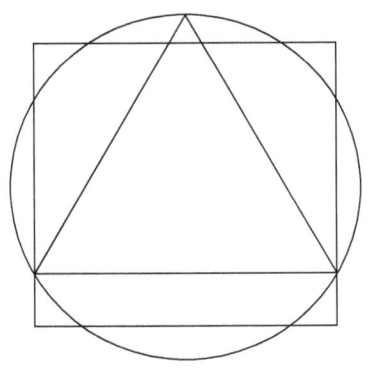

John Michael Greer

AEON

First published in 2025 by
Aeon Books

Copyright © 2025 by John Michael Greer

The right of John Michael Greer to be identified as the author of this work has been asserted in accordance with §§ 77 and 78 of the Copyright Design and Patents Act 1988.

All rights reserved. No part of this publication may be reproduced, stored in a retrieval system, or transmitted, in any form or by any means, electronic, mechanical, photocopying, recording, or otherwise, without the prior written permission of the publisher.

British Library Cataloguing in Publication Data

A C.I.P. for this book is available from the British Library

ISBN-13: 978-1-80152-169-7

Typeset by Medlar Publishing Solutions Pvt Ltd, India

www.aeonbooks.co.uk

Those who think of building a temple in their minds are freed from the sins of a hundred births.
—*Agni-Purana*

CONTENTS

INTRODUCTION	xi
Occultism and religion	xii
Sources of the teachings	xiv
How to use this book	xix
CHAPTER ONE: The first circle	1
Occult anatomy	1
The seven vortices	7
The three exercises	9
Visualizing the temple: Phase one	14
Visualizing your guardian angel	16
The minor orders	17
Completing the first circle	18
CHAPTER TWO: The second circle	19
Visualizing the temple: Phase two	19
The first two vortices	22
Awakening the palm centers	23
The order of Cleric	25
The sacrament of blessing	27

Chewing, nutrition, and exercise	29
Ceremony of commitment for a Cleric	31
Holy water and holy oil	32
Completing the second circle	33

CHAPTER THREE: The third circle — 35

Visualizing the temple: Phase three	35
The third vortex	36
Charging the palm centers	36
The order of Doorkeeper	39
Your work as a Cleric	40
The sacrament of naming	41
Smell and intuition	42
Ceremony of commitment for a Doorkeeper	44
Completing the third circle	45

CHAPTER FOUR: The fourth circle — 47

Visualizing the temple: Phase four	47
The fourth vortex	48
The palm centers and the two currents	49
The order of Reader	51
Your work as a Doorkeeper	53
The sacrament of teaching	54
Ceremony of commitment for a Reader	55
Completing the fourth circle	56

CHAPTER FIVE: The fifth circle — 57

Visualizing the temple: Phase five	57
The fifth vortex	58
Blessing with the palm centers	59
The order of Healer	60
Hearing and intuition	62
Your work as a Reader	64
The sacrament of anointing	64
Ceremony of commitment for a Healer	65
Completing the fifth circle	66

CHAPTER SIX: The sixth circle — 67

Visualizing the temple: Phase six	67

CONTENTS ix

The sixth vortex	68
Self-healing with the palm centers	69
The order of Acolyte	73
Your work as a Healer	75
Life as sacrament	76
Touch and intuition	77
Ceremony of commitment for an Acolyte	79
Completing the sixth circle	81

CHAPTER SEVEN: The seventh circle — 83
- Visualizing the temple: Phase seven — 84
- The seventh vortex — 85
- The circulation of light — 86
- Healing others with the palm centers — 89
- A form of initiation — 94
- Introduction to the communion ceremony — 96
- Requirements of the ceremony — 98
- The communion ceremony — 99
- The temple as mesocosm — 103
- The communion ceremony in group workings — 105
- Completing the seventh circle — 105

CHAPTER EIGHT: Beyond the seven circles — 107
- Books relevant to the Golden Section Fellowship — 108
- Other resources — 110

APPENDIX: *Practices of the golden section fellowship* — 111
- The Sphere of Protection — 111
- Discursive meditation — 118
- Lodge ceremonies — 121
- Spring equinox ceremony — 127
- Summer solstice ceremony — 129
- Autumn equinox ceremony — 131
- Winter solstice ceremony — 133

RESOURCES — 137

INDEX — 139

INTRODUCTION

In a certain sense, occult training is like climbing a mountain. To begin with, a climber attracted by the lure of the peaks must journey up out of the lowlands into the foothills, rising into clearer air and getting a better view of the peak ahead. Thereafter, the climber must approach the mountain itself and scramble up its lower slopes, learning its ways and finding the best available route for the most challenging part of the ascent. Then the last trees fall away, grassy slopes give way to bare rock and glacial ice, and the climber must use all of his or her hard-won skills to ascend, step by step, to the final attainment of the peak.

The first two books in this series, *The Way of the Golden Section* and *The Way of the Four Elements*, correspond to the first two stages of the mountaineer's work. The first introduced the basic teachings and exercises of the system of occult study and practice this series teaches, establishing a foundation for the work to come and giving the attentive reader some idea of the work ahead. The second took the work a step further by introducing a set of initiatory practices based on the four elements of ancient magical lore. Readers who have studied and practiced the material in those two volumes are well prepared to go further in occultism, and this third and final volume in the sequence is meant to provide the necessary teachings and practices so that you may continue that journey.

The material covered in the earlier volumes is essential for success in the work ahead. If you haven't yet worked through the practices in *The Way of the Golden Section* and *The Way of the Four Elements*, completing the work of the first book as far as the initiation ceremony and working through the cycle of elemental practices in the second book at least once, you should plan on setting aside this book until you have finished those necessary preparations. If you have already passed through these preliminary stages, on the other hand, you should be prepared for the material given here. By completing the work of this book after the work of the two previous volumes, you will advance to the third degree of the Golden Section Fellowship.

The Golden Section Fellowship is not an organization of the usual kind. It charges no dues and hands out no certificates. The qualifications for membership are simply your willingness to take on the challenge of following a specific course of occult training. As a student of the material in this book or the earlier volumes in this series, you don't need to submit your work to a mentor, or take classes taught by an instructor. The practices given here are self-correcting and will teach you through experience.

Most occult schools in the past used either correspondence study or in-person teaching to pass on the traditions and practices of occultism. Effective as these methods were, they placed hard limits on how many people could access the teachings of occultism. These books, and several other volumes related to them, are meant to provide an open-source self-study program instead. The practices given in these volumes are designed to be safe and effective to perform on your own, at your own pace. Any necessary cautions are given in detail.

Occultism and religion

Though the work ahead of you has several aspects, much of it has to do with the realms where occultism approaches the borders of religion. To understand this, it may be helpful to start by defining our terms. What, then, is occultism? And what is religion?

The word "occult" comes from a Latin word meaning "hidden." (It has nothing to do with the word "cult.") Centuries ago, during the Renaissance, students of the hidden possibilities of the human mind and spirit, and of spiritual teachings forbidden by the dogmatic churches of the time, took to calling their subjects of study "occult philosophy," that is, "hidden philosophy." Over time that phrased was rounded off to yield the word "occultism." Occultism is the study of consciousness and its powers, of everything in the universe that has more in common with mind than with matter, and of certain traditional practices and philosophies that open the way to direct personal experience of realities beyond the material plane.

The word "religion" also comes from Latin, and its original meaning is "reconnection"—*re-* means the same thing in Latin as it does in English, and *ligio* comes from the verb *ligere*, "to link," and means "a linking, a connection." Religion is the set of teachings and practices that human beings use to restore their linkage with the Divine. Just as science deals with the outer universe of matter and energy, and occultism deals with the inner universe of mind and spirit, religion deals with the divine source of both these universes, and helps human beings reconnect themselves to the source of their being.

Thus occultism is not a religion, and religion is not occult. Certain occult teachings and practices, however, approach the border between these two fields of human experience. Some cultures and religions assign these things to one side of the border between occultism and religion, while some put them on the other side. For example, holy water—water that has been blessed in a ritual manner—is consecrated by priests or other holy people in some places, by occultists in others, and by ordinary people in still others. Does it belong to religion, to occultism, or to something else? That depends on who you ask.

The points just made need to be kept in mind, because this book—and the Golden Section Fellowship generally—approaches these things from the point of view of occultism, not religion. As a student of this material, you remain entirely free to follow the faith of your choice, to worship the Divine under whatever names and forms call to you, and to attend services of any kind you choose. While it is true that the teachings of the Golden Section Fellowship about the afterlife, for example, differ from those taught by some religious denominations, you are not required to believe the teachings these books present—just to think about them and see whether they make sense of your experience of the world.

The teachings and practices in this third stage of the work are intended to help you advance further toward the higher reaches of human spiritual potential. By themselves, given daily practice and a great deal of hard work, they will build on the foundations of the two earlier volumes and give you access to more of your own inner capacities. Combined with the practices of any religion, or simply your own willingness to approach the source of being, they will bring you at least a little closer to the transcendent spiritual realities at the heart of things, and make it at least a little easier to experience those realities for yourself. By doing so, they help you continue the quest at the heart of the Golden Section Fellowship: the quest for wisdom, revelation, and enlightenment.

Sources of the teachings

There are many different traditions, schools, and lineages in Western occultism, just as there are in every other spiritual tradition. While no two branches of occultism have exactly the same teachings and practices to offer, all of them draw on the same shared body of lore, and most of them can trace the origins of the material they teach back through the years to older sources. There's much to be learned by following these threads of occult history back from teacher to teacher and from school to school. Students of this book also quite reasonably may want to know the sources of the material presented here. This is a complex matter, because I have learned from many teachers and schools over the years, and the lore and exercises I have woven together into this book come from many places. I have discussed the most important of these in the paragraphs below.

The Universal Gnostic Church

The Universal Gnostic Church (UGC) was founded in 1952 by Revs. Omar Zasluchy, Owen Symanski, and Matthew Shaw, three ministers of the Universalist Church in Pennsylvania who disagreed with their church's decision to amalgamate with the Unitarian Church. They appreciated the open-minded and tolerant attitudes of their Universalist heritage, but they wished to combine it with a commitment to personal spiritual experience, and they drew much of their inspiration from the example of the ancient Gnostics.

The Gnostics—as my teacher John Gilbert loved to point out, this is pronounced "gnaw sticks"—were a diverse movement of occultists and religious mystics who flourished in the ancient Greek and Roman world, and survived into the Middle Ages despite a rising tide of violent persecution by established churches. Their name comes from the Greek term *gnosis*, a word that is difficult to translate into English. It means "knowledge," but not the kind of knowledge that you can learn in books or pass on in words. Historian of religions Bentley Layton, in his collection of Gnostic scriptures, translated the word gnosis as "acquaintance," because it is the kind of knowledge you have of someone when you become personally acquainted with them.

Central to the teachings of the ancient Gnostics was the belief that gnosis, personal acquaintance with the Divine, is at the heart of the religious quest. That belief was the one thing the diverse Gnostic sects of the time had in common, and it was the aspect of ancient Gnosticism that inspired the founders of the Universal Gnostic Church. Because the original Gnostics traced their spiritual inspiration back to Jesus of Nazareth, the three founders of the church arranged to be consecrated to the historic episcopacy of the Christian church by Bishop Robert Monroe of the Liberal Catholic Church (LCC), an independent sacramental church allied with the Theosophical movement.

The independent sacramental movement, of which the LCC has long been a significant part, would require an entire book to explain; fortunately that book has already been written by John Plummer, a bishop active in that movement.[1] The very short version is that down through the years an assortment of bishops with the right to transmit apostolic succession—the direct lineal connection back to the apostles of Jesus of Nazareth—broke away from the various dogmatic hierarchical churches and became independent. Around them, over the course of the last two centuries, a movement of independent churches has gradually formed, offering various forms of Christian sacramental spirituality to the world. It's a complex, lively scene in which spiritual practice is more important than doctrine and bishops, priests, and priestesses typically behave like servants of the people rather than their masters.

Despite its connection with the independent sacramental movement, the UGC was never exclusively Christian. It revered the Divine which, according to its teachings, is behind all the forms and names of human religions. It welcomed participants of every faith, and it encouraged its members to invoke the Divine under whatever names and forms appealed most to them. The use of the term "the Divine" was standard in the teaching documents of the UGC precisely because it allows for this flexibility, and members of the church were encouraged to replace that generic label with the name or names used for deity within their own tradition.

---

[1] See Plummer (2006) in the *Resources* section at the end of this book.

The founders of the church also crafted the name of their new church with a great deal of care, because they disagreed with certain beliefs common among the ancient Gnostic sects. Some Gnostic teachings, for example, held that some people were capable of attaining gnosis while others were not; some Gnostics likewise taught that the universe was a prison from which souls had to escape. By contrast, Zasluchy, Symanski, and Shaw envisioned a *universal gnosis*—that is, a spiritual path accessible to everyone—and a *gnosis of the universe*—a spiritual vision that experienced the Divine in all things, including the material plane of existence.

While Bishops Zasluchy and Symanski remained in Pennsylvania, Shaw moved to Colorado, where he became an associate of the occult teacher Dr. Juliet Ashley, and developed a series of seven Gnostic Lessons for students of the UGC teachings. In 1984 he consecrated several new bishops of the UGC, John Gilbert among them. John and several other UGC bishops later received consecration *sub conditione* from Bishop Warren Smith in 1994, receiving from him many other lines of apostolic succession.[2] In 2004, John and two other UGC bishops, Rima Laibow and Albert Stubblebine, passed on the same consecration to me. John and his fellow bishops also consecrated a few other people in the UGC lineage, but the organization gradually wound up after 2010, when John retired.[3]

In the UGC as I knew it, an important part of the training available to members was the set of seven Gnostic Lessons mentioned above, which taught basic elements of the church's vision and path. These also provided instruction in spiritual practices, and conferred the five minor orders the UGC offered: Cleric, Doorkeeper, Reader, Healer, and Acolyte. In earlier centuries, the minor orders were important in many of the historic churches, but they have largely fallen out of use in modern times. This is unfortunate, because the minor orders bridge the gap between ordinary lay members and the priesthood, and provide important lessons and opportunities for those who are not (or are not yet) prepared to take priestly vows.

The priesthood of the Universal Gnostic Church can only be passed on by personal ordination including the laying on of hands, and the consecration of bishops in the UGC has similar but even more

---

[2] Consecration *sub conditione* is a ceremony used when there is any question of the validity of a bishop's consecration; it is in effect a re-consecration in case the first was invalid. It has seen much use in the independent sacramental movement to reunite the scattered lines of apostolic succession.

[3] As of this writing, it is in the process of being revived from dormancy.

complex requirements. The Gnostic Lessons, on the other hand, were routinely passed on in mimeographed or photocopied form by mail in the twentieth century, and via web pages online in the early twenty-first century. I have therefore included a lightly revised and expanded version of the Gnostic Lessons in this book, and used them as the basic framework for the course of studies given here.

I have also included another set of teachings from the Universal Gnostic tradition, a set of exercises for awakening the energy centers in the palms for the purpose of healing, blessing, and initiation. These originally came from Bishop Matthew Shaw, who taught them to many of his students, John Gilbert among them; where Shaw got them is a mystery I have not yet been able to solve. They use the same elemental symbols as the Sphere of Protection and can be activated and used in various ways, some of which are discussed in my other books.

American occult teachings

During the years when I studied with John Gilbert, I also pursued a series of research projects into the history of American occultism. Those two processes were closely related, because it became clear to me very early in my studies with John that what he had received from his teachers consisted of fragments drawn from some larger system. My goal was to recover as much as possible of the wider context of the UGC and the initiatory orders associated with it—the Ancient Order of Druids in America, the Holy Order of the Golden Dawn, the Modern Order of Essenes, and the Order of Spiritual Alchemy.

Progress was slow at first, but as a steady stream of old occult literature found its way into online archives, I was able to gather more of the raw material I needed. Among the most useful sources were the writings of Harry J. Gardener, an occultist active in Los Angeles in the middle years of the twentieth century, who published complete instructions for certain secret practices in his many mimeographed publications. Another important source of help was a Rosicrucian order, the Societas Rosicruciana in America (SRIA), which included a great deal of otherwise inaccessible information in its correspondence courses.[4] The books of the SRIA's former head George Winslow Plummer were also of considerable assistance.

---

[4] This is not the same organization as the larger and better-advertised Rosicrucian order AMORC, of which I have never been a member.

One of the things that made these teachings especially interesting and useful to me is that they anchor spiritual practice in the occult dimensions of human anatomy. A century ago this was a central theme of occult instruction. Students of the occult in those days knew about the endocrine glands, the sympathetic nervous system, and the cerebrospinal fluid, and developed exercises that worked with these things to achieve expanded states of consciousness. While that knowledge has been misplaced in more recent occult systems, much of it has been preserved in print, and I was able to uncover a great deal of instruction on these topics and test it out.

I have already published some of this material in *The Secret of the Five Rites* (Aeon Books, 2024), and a great deal more still awaits testing and publication. Several practices I found in the course of these explorations, however, fit smoothly into gaps in the material I learned from John Gilbert, resulting in a more complete system of occult training and spiritual development. After extensive testing, I included some of these practices, along with the theory that explains them, in this sequence of training.

Expanding the tradition in this way was standard practice in the days when the UGC flourished. Matthew Shaw launched an organization of his own, the Modern Order of Essenes, to teach certain healing practices that complement the UGC teachings. Several other organizations that had originally been independent of the UGC—the Ancient Order of Druids in America, the Holy Order of the Golden Dawn, and the Order of Spiritual Alchemy—also affiliated with the church along these lines. Under John Gilbert's leadership, several of the bishops he consecrated founded their own Fellowships along similar lines. At the time, I was busy reviving the Ancient Order of Druids in America and so did not create a Fellowship; the Golden Section Fellowship may be considered my contribution to this part of the tradition.

The temple tradition

The third principal source of the material in this book, the one that gives it its name, has a more complex origin. Many years ago, in the course of extensive studies into folklore and occultism, I became aware that traditions in many lands assign a curious power to temples, churches, and other sacred places built according to particular sacred geometries and used in specific ways: they were held to increase crop fertility in the land immediately around them. Years of research into these legends, the mostly forgotten teachings behind them, and ancient methods of agriculture convinced me that there once existed an archaic folk technology, which I call the temple technology, that used naturally occurring energies to boost plant growth.

My book *The Secret of the Temple* documented what I was able to uncover about the temple technology. A second book, *The Ceremony of the Grail*, extended the investigation into certain dimensions of the history of occultism and Freemasonry. My investigations in this field continue and other books on the subject will doubtless result from it.

In the course of this research, however, I also came into contact with the many other roles that temples, real and imagined, play in occult spirituality. To some extent that came as no surprise—as a Freemason, for example, I have long been familiar with the place of the Temple of Solomon in Masonic symbolism—but some of the things I found opened unexpected doors and introduced me to dimensions of occult practice I had not previously considered. Much of this fed into the work that resulted in this book.

The secret temple mentioned in the title of this book is not a material building. In one sense, it is a temple created in the mind through a process of sustained visualization. In another sense, it is the human body, the fundamental measure of all traditional architecture and the basis for certain essential occult practices taught in this book. In a third sense it is the Golden Section Fellowship itself, a structure you have been building in your own mind and spirit by the studies and practices you have pursued to this point. As you proceed through this book, the secret temple in all these senses will be a recurring theme in the work.

How to use this book

The Way of the Secret Temple is intended for students of occultism who have learned the basic and intermediate practices of the occult path and are ready to go further—to build on the foundation that the studies and practical work of the two previous books have established. It is not a book for beginners. So long as you have already worked through the material in the previous Golden Section Fellowship books, however, you are ready to proceed with the material in this book. A summary of the Golden Section practices that are used in this book is included in the Appendix for reference.

The material that follows is divided into seven circles. Each of these has its own set of studies and practices, which will take at least a month to complete and may take as much more time as you feel you need to master the material in each circle. The period of seven months or more you spend on this book will initiate you into the third degree of the Golden Section Fellowship, but it will also give you a set of practices that you can use for the rest of your life in the quest for wisdom, revelation, and enlightenment.

The work of each circle builds on the circles before it, so the whole sequence should be done in order, starting with the first page of the first circle and proceeding from there. The practices you have already learned in your previous studies in the Golden Section Fellowship should be continued, though certain modifications to those practices will be covered as we proceed. Additional exercises will also be assigned. You can therefore expect to spend around one hour a day, every day, to complete the work of this book.

As with the previous volumes in this series, you will need to keep a practice record—a journal, diary, or daybook in which you note down each day's practices and their results. By now, if you have been keeping up with this part of the work, your practice journal will cover a great many months of practices. If you've let this slip, consider starting again, beginning now. Some of the uses of your practice journal will be brought up later in this book.

If you are prepared to commit the necessary time and energy to the work, we can proceed to the first of the circles.

CHAPTER ONE

The first circle

The foundation of your work in all seven circles of this book is the set of basic practices introduced in *The Way of the Golden Section*: the morning and evening exercises, the solar plexus exercise, divination, the initiates' version of the Sphere of Protection ritual, and discursive meditation. As discussed in that earlier book, these practices are to be done daily. With very few exceptions, the practices introduced in this book are done in addition to those, rather than instead of them. These practices form the foundation of the secret temple you will be building and empowering over the months to come.

This first circle introduces certain modifications to your daily meditation practice, as well as a new daily exercise. In order to make sense of these additions, some background in the occult dimensions of the human body will be helpful.

Occult anatomy

Very few people in today's occult community remember that the anatomy of the human body was once an important subject of study among occultists. Many occult schools required their members to pay attention to human anatomy, and study it closely, and some included detailed lessons on occult anatomy in their study courses. Even those who did not go quite so far expected students to know their way around the structures of the human body. Manly P. Hall, the most influential American occult teacher of the twentieth century, thus listed a textbook of anatomy as the very first entry on his list of essential literature for the occult student.[5]

There are several good reasons for this. One of the core concepts of occult tradition is the recognition that everything we experience with our material senses is a reflection of realities in the Unseen. "The visible is the manifestation of the invisible": in these words Eliphas Lévi, whose writings launched the modern occult revival, expressed what he called the only doctrine of magic. This link between the Seen and the Unseen is as true of the human body as it is of any other material thing, and occultists in the past thus paid close attention to anatomy as a way to understand certain aspects of the subtle bodies of humanity.

There is a more practical issue to occult anatomy, however. Three systems in the human body—the sympathetic nervous system, the endocrine system, and the cerebrospinal fluid—all play significant roles in the states of expanded awareness that occult practices are meant to awaken. A fourth part of the body, the vagus nerve, weaves these three together and provides a gentle but effective means of acting on them using the tools of the operative occultist. All these details of anatomy have effects on consciousness that can be put to good use in the quest for wisdom, revelation, and enlightenment. A survey of the occult anatomy of the body will help you understand important aspects of the work ahead.

The sympathetic nervous system

Most people these days finish their schooling with a vague notion that the human nervous system centers in the brain and spreads from there through the spinal cord to connect with the body. This is accurate enough but incomplete, because it only describes one of the two nervous systems your body has: the cerebrospinal nervous system, to give it its proper name. The other is the sympathetic nervous system, and it

---

[5] Hall (1925, p. 53). Gray's *Anatomy* (Gray 1978) is the one recommended to me by my occult teachers.

has a crucial part to play in the activities of daily life as well as the work of the occultist.

Where the cerebrospinal nervous system is centralized in the brain and spinal cord, the sympathetic nervous system is more diffuse. It comprises more than a dozen plexuses—little brains, in effect—which are located in various parts of the body, and are linked together by a network of nerves that function independently of the brain and spinal cord. The largest of the plexuses is the solar plexus, which is located behind the stomach and in front of the spine, and is about the size and complexity of a cat's brain.

Other important plexuses in the sympathetic nervous system are the two cardiac plexuses, one in front of the heart and one behind it; the hypogastric plexus, below the stomach; and the pelvic plexus, at the bottom of the pelvic basin, between the sex organs and the rectum. Each of these is divided into many smaller masses of nerve cells, and each of them connects with the vital organs in the body core.

The sympathetic nervous system has many functions in the body. From the point of view of the operative occultist, however, its main importance is that it is the material basis of the subjective mind. Occult teachers have recognized since ancient times that each of us has two minds, the objective mind and the subjective mind. The former is the mind that looks outward at the world of objects, and it is centered in the brain and the cerebrospinal nervous system more generally; the subjective mind is the mind that looks inward at your experience as a subject, and it is centered in the solar plexus and the sympathetic nervous system more generally.

For centuries now, the cultures of the Western world have focused all their attention on the objective mind and its experiences, and ignored and dismissed the subjective mind and the very different world of experiences it has to offer. That one-sided approach is unbalanced and it leads to many problems that afflict people today. As you learned in *The Way of the Golden Section*, the objective mind makes you a unique individual, while the subjective mind makes you one with the universe. The insights of the objective mind are thus essential, but they need to be balanced by the insights of the subjective mind. One of the exercises discussed below is meant to help further the process of restoring your access to your own subjective mind, and all the exercises in the circles ahead will contribute to that process.

The endocrine system

Another system that plays an important though too often neglected role in human consciousness is the endocrine system, which consists of a set of small glands scattered throughout the body. Also called the ductless glands, the endocrine glands release chemicals that have powerful effects on body and consciousness alike. Sometimes these effects are obvious. For example, the testicles and ovaries are endocrine glands, and produce the hormones involved in sexual arousal; another set of endocrine glands are the adrenal glands, which sit on top of your kidneys, and release adrenaline into the body to give you a sudden rush of energy when you are stressed or facing a challenge.

Like the sympathetic nervous system, the endocrine system is a network rather than a centralized structure. Each of the endocrine glands influences all the others, and is influenced by them in turn. Two of them, however, have special importance in maintaining the balance of chemicals in the bloodstream: the pituitary gland and the pineal gland.

The pituitary gland is located under the front of the brain, behind the root of the nose and between the two temples. About the size of a shelled almond, it is dark reddish-brown in color, and divided into two lobes, one behind the other. It releases hormones that keep the rest of the endocrine glands in balance. These are so important for maintaining health that removal of the pituitary gland causes death within three days.

The pineal gland is further back in the head; if you put your fingertips at the top of your ears, where the ear tissue joins the head, the pineal gland is roughly between them. It is reddish-gray and about the size of a grain of rice. Weirdly, though it is as far from light as anything in the head can be, it still has the basic structure of an eye, and evolutionary biologists have shown that it is descended from a third eye, located in the top of the head, possessed by some ancient fish and reptiles. Its role in body chemistry is still not well understood by medical researchers, although it is known to produce melatonin, a chemical that encourages sound sleep.

Occult researchers have studied these two glands carefully for centuries, because both of them have powers and properties that today's medical science does not recognize. The pituitary gland is the "third eye" of Eastern mystical teachings; in Western traditions, it is identified as the organ of clairvoyant vision, and symbolically associated with the Sun. It provides the human mind with its anchor point in the material body. When awakened through occult practices, it is the center through which the will is energized and activated by the mind.

The pineal gland relates to the spirit rather than the mind, and provides the higher, spiritual functions of the human self with one of their two anchor points in the material body. (The other is the solar plexus.) The pineal gland is also an eye, but it functions on a higher level than the "third eye"; in some Eastern traditions it is called the eye of Dangma, while certain Western traditions call it the Eye of Revelation. It is symbolically associated with the Moon.

When the pineal gland is gently stimulated in certain specific ways, it releases a compound that has powerful effects on the endocrine system, mostly by way of the pituitary gland. Both glands are able to put chemicals into the bloodstream, but they also have a more direct connection between them. The pineal gland is located in the third ventricle, an open space filled with fluid on the underside of the brain. An extension of the third ventricle, called the infundibulum, reaches forward and down to the pituitary gland, allowing compounds released into the third ventricle to reach the pituitary gland directly.

The cerebrospinal fluid

There are five ventricles in the brain, which allow fluid to reach most parts of the brain directly. The fluid that moves through them also flows around the outside of the brain. It fills the space between the brain and the membranes that line the inside of the skull, and it also flows down a channel in the middle of the spinal cord, reaching down to the level of the solar plexus. This fluid, the cerebrospinal fluid, helps support the delicate tissues of the brain and protect it against shocks, but it has subtler functions as well.

It needs to be understood first of all that the bloodstream is only one of the ways that hormones and other body and brain chemicals circulate through the body. Weaving through the whole body alongside the blood vessels are another set of vessels, the lymph channels, which drain excess fluid from the system and also help the immune system get antibodies and protective cells where they need to go. There is also the interstitial fluid, which has no channels of its own but moves through the spaces between cells throughout the body, carrying body chemicals with it. Finally there is the cerebrospinal fluid, which has similar functions in the central nervous system.

In children, all these fluids flow freely. In many adults, by contrast, the lymph, the interstitial fluid and the cerebrospinal fluid become stagnant, so that body and brain chemicals cannot reach everywhere they should, and pockets of fluids become trapped here and there, causing various health problems. This is an important source of the problems of old age, and it also interferes with certain advanced spiritual practices. Many of the exercises practiced by occultists and mystics are designed to get the fluids moving again.

This is especially important in those forms of occult practice that work with the pineal and pituitary glands. In order to get the most benefit from practices of this kind, it is vital to have a reasonably free flow of cerebrospinal fluid, especially but not only through the third ventricle of the brain. One of the exercises given below is designed to help with this.

The vagus nerve

Connecting all three of the systems we have just discussed is the vagus nerve. Most nerves that connect the brain to the body go through the spinal cord, but the vagus nerve is the exception. It leaves the underside of the brain in two cords, one on each side of the neck, and then spreads out to make contact with most of the body's vital organs, many of the endocrine glands, and most of the plexuses of the sympathetic nervous system, including the solar plexus. It is the equivalent in your material body of the channel connecting the solar plexus and the pineal gland, which you learned to visualize in the initiate's version of the Sphere of Protection (introduced toward the end of *The Way of the Golden Section*).

What makes the vagus nerve especially important is that it allows changes in the body to stimulate changes in the brain, and vice versa, without having to go through the complicated filters of the central nervous system. It is in this way that physical exercises can affect your thoughts and feelings, and thoughts and feelings can influence the health of your body. The rhythmic breathing you learned to practice early on in your occult studies made use of this effect, sending impulses up the vagus nerve to influence the brain. The visualizations you have practiced all through your occult training also used the same effect, sending influences down the vagus nerve to influence the body.

At this stage of your occult training, more direct ways to work with the vagus nerve can be emphasized. One of these ways, the solar plexus exercise, has already been part of your work since you began practicing the material in *The Way of the Golden Section*. This and two other exercises will be fundamental to the work ahead.

The seven vortices

The plexuses, glands, and nerve networks just discussed all belong to the material plane. They are paired, however, with a set of subtle organs or energy centers that belong to the next two planes of occult tradition, the etheric and astral planes—the plane of life force and concrete consciousness, respectively. Just as the material body has organs which fulfill various functions, the etheric and astral bodies have centers of force which have functions of their own. These are the energy centers discussed in occult and mystical writings.

There are many energy centers in the human body—according to some Asian traditions, 360 of them. Most systems of inner development choose some subset of these centers and use those centers as the basis for certain kinds of inner work. Some teachings use only a single center. In many Chinese, Korean, and Japanese martial arts schools, for example, the dantien or hara (located 2 inches below the navel) is the focus of inner work, while most Christian traditions focus attention on the heart alone. On the other end of the spectrum are systems of inner development that work with dozens of energy centers.

Most traditions, however, fall in-between these extremes. The Golden Section Fellowship is among the traditions that take up positions in the middle ground. In *The Way of the Golden Section*, you were introduced to two energy centers: the solar plexus and the pineal gland. In the present volume you will continue to work with these two, but you will add six more centers and take up a new mode of energy work.

These six centers and a seventh located in the area of the pineal gland are referred to as the seven vortices. Each vortex, as the word suggests, is a spinning, spiraling structure of subtle energies anchored to the material body, but also active in the etheric and astral bodies. The more freely and rapidly each vortex spins, the healthier you are in body, mind, and spirit. Regular practice concentrating on the vortices will help them spin freely, benefiting you on all the planes of being.

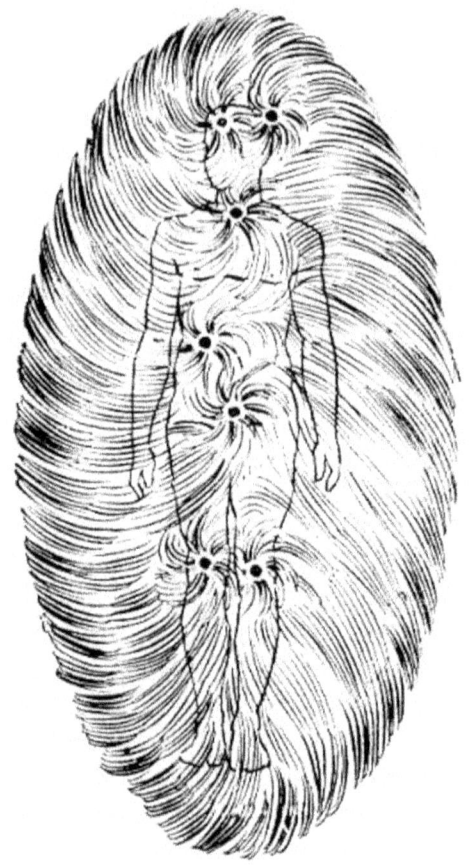

Seven vortices

The seven vortices are shown in the diagram above. They are located as follows:

1. and 2. Behind each kneecap, in the knee joint
3. In the genital area, just above and inward from the base of the penis or clitoris
4. In the right side of the trunk, in the area of the liver
5. At the base of the throat, just above and behind the notch in the collarbone
6. In the middle of the skull, in the place of the pineal gland
7. Behind the root of the nose, a little forward of the pituitary gland

These vortices, obviously enough, are not the same as the seven spinal centers or chakras used in many Asian traditions of spirituality and occultism, most of which are located along the backbone. They are also not the same as the five centers of the Middle Pillar, which are used in some Western magical traditions, or the three cauldrons that play a similar role in some forms of Druid practice; these are located along the midline of the body. Six of the seven vortices are on the front of the body, and the one that isn't, the sixth vortex at the pineal gland, is only about halfway back through the head.

Why the difference? Once again, there are many energy centers in the human body, and many different sets of them can be chosen for spiritual development. Each center has its own effects on the material, etheric, and astral bodies when awakened through inner practice, and each system of spiritual development makes use of those effects in its own ways. In the quest for wisdom, revelation, and enlightenment central to the work of the Golden Section Fellowship, the activation of the seven vortices provides a great deal of help.

The specific function of each vortex is best learned by experience. As you awaken them over the months ahead, you will notice changes in your material and subtle bodies, and those will help guide you to a sense of their effects. As you begin work with the vortices in the head, certain higher functions of consciousness will begin to show themselves, and in due time those will make it easy for you to sense what each vortex does. A few notes have been included in the pages ahead to give you some guidance for the time being.

During the time you spend on the first circle, simply familiarize yourself with the locations of the seven vortices. You will begin the process of awakening them in the practices of the second circle.

The three exercises

These three exercises all work with the vagus nerve, and thus stimulate both the brain and the sympathetic nervous system. They also work with the fluids inside the body to help clear away blockages that can interfere with health and also with the subtler influences of the endocrine glands. The first exercise, the solar plexus exercise, you have already learned and practiced many times; it is repeated below for ease of reference, and its effects are explained in more detail. The other two, the rising call exercise and the energy-awakening exercise, are introduced here for the first time in this sequence of training. The first of them is an independent exercise, which may be done at any time during the day; the second replaces the relaxation and breathing phases of your daily meditation practice.

These exercises should be made part of your daily practice one at a time. First, review the instructions for the solar plexus exercise, and adjust your practice as needed if you have forgotten any of the details. Then, when you are ready, add the rising call exercise to your daily practices, and work with it until you are comfortable with it. Then add the energy-awakening exercise, and proceed from there.

The solar plexus exercise

This exercise should be very familiar to you by now. It was taught early on in *The Way of the Golden Section* and is one of the basic practices of the Golden Section Fellowship. It was once practiced by many people in the occult community, and in Western society in general, as an aid to improved health. Like so many other Western occult practices, however, it dropped out of common use when Asian disciplines such as yoga became popular in the 1960s. It is well worth bringing back into regular use.

This exercise should be practiced every day. It can be done at any convenient time during the day, but only on an empty stomach. It is done as follows:

First, sit in a comfortable chair or sofa, or lie face up on a bed. Take a few moments to relax as much as you can. Then draw in a deep breath and push out your stomach as you do so. This allows you to draw the air down into the very bottom of your lungs.

Second, without breathing out, suck your belly in and push your chest out, moving the air from the lower to the upper part of your lungs. Push your belly out again and let your chest fall, sending the air back down. Do this twice more, so that you've sent the air from the lower lungs to the upper lungs and back again, without breathing out. Then, finally, let the breath out. Let yourself go completely limp, and breathe slowly and comfortably for a little while.

Third, repeat the same sequence—breathing in, sending the air up and back three times, and breathing out—twice more, so you have done the whole sequence three times, relaxing and breathing easily between each sequence.

Fourth, when you have finished, draw in and let out three slow gentle breaths. As you do so, turn your attention to your solar plexus: the center of your subjective mind, the mass of nerve tissue just below your ribcage and just behind your stomach. Imagine it shining warm and golden, like a little sun inside you. Feel the golden light spreading all through your body. When you have finished the three breaths, let go of the image. This concludes the practice.

The solar plexus exercise has four effects important in occult training. First, it helps relax chronic tensions in the body core, which encourages deep breathing and the free flow of the life force. Second, it gives a gentle internal massage to the solar plexus, activating both the nerves and the channels of life force in that important center. Third, the same gentle internal massage helps clear away blockages in the intestines, benefiting your general health.

It is the fourth effect that is most relevant to this stage of your training. Most of your body's endocrine glands are located in your torso, between the base of your neck and the base of your spine. All these glands release chemicals into your interstitial fluids—the fluids that flow between the cells—as well as into the bloodstream.

The internal massage carried out by the solar plexus exercise gets your interstitial fluids flowing freely, dispersing pockets of stagnant fluid and making sure that the secretions of your endocrine glands can spread everywhere they should go. This benefits your health in general, and also allows the special secretions of your pineal and pituitary glands to have their full effect throughout your body.

The rising call exercise

The solar plexus exercise just given was typically taught to beginners. The rising call exercise was introduced to occult students at a more advanced level of training. It has similar effects to the solar plexus exercise, but the internal massage it provides is to the brain and its surrounding tissues. Using posture and breath, it gently increases the pressure of the cerebrospinal fluid and then lets the pressure decrease again. This helps foster the normal circulation of fluid around the brain and through the ventricles, and allows waste products and excess concentrations of brain chemicals to be cleared away. Many people find that this improves their mental clarity and focus.

Like the solar plexus exercise, the rising call exercise should be practiced every day. It can be done at any convenient time during the day, but always on an empty stomach. It is done as follows:

First, standing erect, place the right thumb against the right nostril, allowing the index fingers to extend upward in line with the forehead and leaving the other fingers loose. Now, breathing in through the left nostril, fill the lungs with air completely. Then with the bent middle finger of the same hand close the left nostril also.

Second, with the lungs filled and the lips partly open so that there will be no pressure in the mouth, bend forward from the waist, getting the head lowered as far as is conveniently possible. Then close your mouth and allow a portion of the air in the lungs to gently come back into the nose so as to create just a very slight pressure there. The position allows the blood to flow into every part of the brain and increases the blood pressure slightly. Along with the air pressure, this sets the cerebrospinal fluid in motion, clearing away stagnant pockets of fluid and getting chemicals from the pineal and pituitary glands to every part of the brain. It has a very energizing effect upon the entire system and especially upon the sensitive nerve centers of the brain.

Third, when the desire to resume breathing is quite strong, rise to the erect position, then close the left nostril and allow the breath to escape through the right nostril by moving the thumb. Do not force it out with great speed; nor should you retard it to any great extent. Just let it flow out freely and naturally until the lungs are emptied, without trying to push out the last particle of air through sheer force.

Fourth, with no intervening breaths—in other words, with the very next inhalation of air—repeat the process. Close the right nostril with the right thumb; inhale through the left nostril; close both nostrils; bend forward until ready to exhale; then stand erect; remove the thumb from the right nostril and exhale. Do the complete sequence—breathing in, bending forward, rising, and letting go of the breath—three times. This concludes the practice.

It is important not to do this exercise more than three times, once a day. It has powerful effects and should not be overdone!

The energy-awakening exercise

This exercise is also meant to be done daily, but it fills a somewhat different place in your practice schedule. Up to this point, you have been starting your meditation practice every day with a brief period of relaxation, followed by five minutes of rhythmic breathing. At this stage of your training, you will replace this with a more complex set of preparations.

First, sit in the same position you have been using for meditation all along: seated in a chair far enough forward that your back does not rest against the back of the chair, with your body comfortably poised, your hands on your thighs, and your feet flat on the ground. Draw and release three slow, gentle breaths, allowing any excess tension to flow out of you.

Second, pause briefly. You will be adding certain additional practices at this point in the exercise, as explained below and in later circles.

Third, using the fingertips and thumbs of both hands, gently massage the back of the head and neck for a minute or so. This releases blockages that can interfere with the work you are beginning to do.

Fourth, concentrate on the pineal center, which is located in the center of your head, roughly between the tops of your ears. Imagine light streaming from it, to fill the back of your head with brilliance. The light may be of any color that occurs to you naturally.

Fifth, imagine the light flowing down your spinal column all the way to the base of your spine, then over to your left leg and all the way down to the sole of your left foot. Imagine the light pooling there, as though it is filling your leg up from the bottom of your sole. As the light fills your foot, tense every muscle in your foot; as it fills your lower leg, tense every muscle there; as it fills your thigh, tense every muscle there, until your entire left leg from hip to toes is tensed and full of light. Don't tense the muscles so hard that they tremble, but they should be engaged and active.

Sixth, do exactly the same thing with the right leg, sending a current of light from the back of your head down your spine to the base, and then over and down to the sole of your right foot. Tense your right leg a little at a time as it fills with light. Keep your left leg tense as you do this. By the end of this stage both your legs should be tensed and full of light.

Seventh, do the same thing to your torso from the base up to the level of the armpits, filling it with light and tensing the muscles. Then send the current of light down your left arm to the fingertips, filling the arm a little at a time with light and tensing the muscles. Then do the same thing with your right arm. Finally, bring the light up to fill your shoulders, your neck, and your head and face, tensing these as well. By the time the light reaches the crown of your head, your entire body should be tense and full of light from top to bottom.

Eighth, relax the tensions in the order you established them, beginning with the left foot and leg, then the right foot and leg, then the torso to the armpits, and so on. As you relax the muscles, keep the awareness of the light filling your body. As you end this phase, your muscles are relaxed and your whole body is full of the light that radiated from your pineal gland.

Ninth, proceed with your meditation in the usual way, beginning or ending with a prayer if this is your usual practice.

This exercise has several functions. The tensing of the body from the feet upward, followed by relaxation, helps you shed unnecessary tensions. It also does the same thing to the entire body that the solar plexus exercise does to the torso and the rising call exercise does to the brain and its surrounding membranes: it gives the whole structure a gentle massage to release blockages and get the fluids flowing freely In this way it helps preserve and improve health, lifts some of the burdens of age, and enables the chemicals released by the pineal and pituitary glands to spread freely through the body.

Meanwhile, the visualization of light moving through the body is not arbitrary or pointless. The connection made by the vagus nerve between the brain and the sympathetic nervous system gives symbolic imagery the power to affect the material body directly, while your imagination has more direct effects on your etheric and astral bodies, the bodies of life force and concrete consciousness. As you practice this exercise—and especially once you add certain further exercises which will be introduced in later circles—you will find that these subtler bodies will be awakened and energized by this practice.

Visualizing the temple: Phase one

Along with the third exercise just given, there are two other additions to your daily meditation practice that need to be introduced at this point in your work. Both of them are visualizations. One of them will be done at the beginning of your meditation work each day, and the other at the end.

The first of these draws from the temple tradition that was mentioned in the introduction to this book, and is explained in more detail in my books *The Secret of the Temple* and *The Ceremony of the Grail*. That tradition focused primarily on temples that were actually built in the material world, but occultists in several branches of the tradition learned that a temple built up in the imagination—that is, in occult terms, on the astral plane—can be put to work in the quest for spiritual development.

How this works is best explained once you have experienced the process for yourself, and will be covered in the chapter on the seventh circle.

I have used the word "temple" in this book, but it should be noted that the same teachings and traditions were incorporated into a very wide range of religious structures, extending all the way from Christian churches in medieval Ireland to Shinto shrines in Japan. Feel free to envision the structure you are building in accordance with your own religious beliefs—that is to say, make it a church or chapel if you are a Christian, a synagogue if you are a Jew, and so on. The secret temple you are building is yours and yours alone, and should reflect your personal needs and values. The shape and design of the building, however, should follow the descriptions given in this book exactly.

In earlier times, when temples, churches, and other holy places were built and used as resonating chambers for subtle natural energies and formed magical and spiritual connections between the material world and the Unseen, they were not simply put up haphazardly in any convenient location. Only certain sites where the natural energies were especially strong were suitable locations for a temple. Once a prospective site had been located by various means, including divination and the reading of omens, the master builder in charge of the project might put many hours into sitting quietly at the location, watching the behavior of birds and animals, observing the movements of clouds and winds, and sensing the movements of the Unseen in that place, before the first stone was brought to the site or the first spade was thrust into the ground.

This is what you will be doing in your imagination before you begin each session of meditation. Once you take your seat, during the pause that marks the second step of the energy-awakening exercise, imagine yourself sitting on a wooden chair in a field beneath the open sky. It can be any landscape that appeals to you. It should include a relatively flat area in which you are seated, and on which your own secret temple will be built; this can be as large or as small as you desire.

As you imagine yourself in the place, see the grass or soil beneath you, the landscape around you, the sky above; if the Sun is shining, feel its warmth, and if not, feel the chill in the air; feel and smell the breeze blowing past you. Here as always, don't worry about whether or not you can see the imaginary scene in the right way; there is no right way. Imagine it, and be present as vividly as you can in the imagined landscape.

Do this for five minutes or so, and then proceed to the rest of the energy-awakening exercise and from there to your meditation. Once you have finished the work of the first circle and are ready to proceed to the second, you will change this visualization in certain specific ways, as your inner temple takes its next step toward completion.

Visualizing your guardian angel

One of the teachings that occultism shares with many religions is the belief that every human soul has a spiritual guardian. In Christianity and Judaism, this being is called the guardian angel, while in the Pagan faiths of the ancient world it was called the guardian genius if it was associated with a man, and the guardian juno if it was a woman's.[6] The term "guardian angel" will be used in this book, but under all these names, Western occult teachings place much focus on making contact with your protective and guiding spirit.

There are many ways to accomplish this work. None of them are easy, because of the gap that separates the material plane where human consciousness is focused from the higher planes where angelic beings exist. The most common methods taught in modern occult schools require many hours a day for spiritual exercises, and require a period of between six and eighteen months devoted entirely to the work, with the rest of your life put on hold. Many people have mundane responsibilities that will not permit them to do this.

In the tradition I inherited from the Universal Gnostic Church, by contrast, the work is carried out more gradually but also more gently as part of the normal sequence of daily practices. This approach is not as rapid as the more common method, but it can be done by anyone who can spare the time for occult practice at all. It also avoids the risk of psychological imbalance, which the more intensive methods can sometimes cause.

The method is simple—which does not, of course, mean that it is easy! Once you have finished your meditation, before you go on to the closing self-massage, imagine your guardian angel (or guardian genius, or guardian juno) standing in front of you. Picture it as a human figure with

---

[6] The word "genius" meant "good spirit" long before it took on its modern meaning of a very talented person.

angel wings, dressed in a white robe.[7] The other details are entirely up to you. Imagine it as clearly as you can. If you feel drawn to do so, you may speak to it. The important thing, however, is to imagine it being present with you. Once you have held the image for a few minutes, thank your guardian angel, release the image, and go on to the closing self-massage.

The first few times you do this, it will accomplish very little. This is why you will be doing this practice every single day after your meditation. The image you create is not your guardian angel, but it sends a signal into the Unseen asking for contact with your guardian, and provides a vehicle on the astral plane that your guardian angel can use to communicate with you. Day by day, as you persevere in this practice, your guardian angel will be able to guide you more easily, and long before you perceive its communications in any conscious manner you will notice that your hunches and intuitive glimpses are clearer and provide better guidance.

This is not a fast process, though. If you have ever had the experience of using an old-fashioned radio receiver, you know that it can take a great deal of fiddling with the knobs to get the signal you want to come through clearly! The same thing is true, in effect, with your guardian angel: it will take you time and patience to pick up on the messages that it sends you. Years, in all probability, will pass before the communication becomes easy and clear. As with so much of practical occultism, time and steady practice are needed to accomplish the work.

Your guardian angel cannot make you do anything, and it will never try to command you. Since you have free will, it can only offer advice and show you things from its wider perspective. That is why it has to wait for you to make the effort to reach out to it. If you seem to be getting a message ordering you around, or telling you to do something that goes against your conscience or your values, you have tuned into the wrong station, so to speak. Keep up your daily practices, and use prayer and divination to orient yourself so you can make the right contact.

The minor orders

The three exercises, the temple visualization, and the guardian angel visualization, along with the basic practices already given, are fundamental to the work of this book and should be continued daily through

---

[7] If your religious beliefs do not permit you to imagine the angel in this form, simply imagine a formless, conscious presence.

the time you spend working through the seven circles. The remaining work ahead of you will vary from month to month. Most of the practices you will take up as you proceed come from the Gnostic Lessons, the traditional training program for the minor orders of the Universal Gnostic Church.

What are minor orders? In many traditional churches, they are offices that can be filled by laypeople who are prepared to pass through a certain amount of training, without the lifelong commitments that are involved in becoming a priest. Different churches have different minor orders. In the UGC, there are five minor orders: Cleric, Doorkeeper, Reader, Healer, and Acolyte. It was traditional for candidates for the priesthood or priestesshood of the UGC to pass through all the minor orders before beginning the long process of preparation for ordination, but during the heyday of the UGC ordinary members were also encouraged to study the Gnostic Lessons and receive the minor orders.[8]

As a Gnostic church, the UGC tradition put personal spiritual experience and the freedom of the individual at the center of its value system. Studying the Gnostic Lessons and receiving the minor orders of the UGC does not require you to leave any existing religious organization or tradition to which you may belong, nor does it commit you to follow the UGC tradition afterwards. The commitments you make and the practices you take up are entirely between you and the Divine as you know and experience it.

Completing the first circle

Plan on devoting at least one month to learning and practicing the work of this circle. Before you go on to the next circle, review all the material assigned to the first circle and be sure you understand it and have practiced it correctly. Each circle that follows depends for its effect on the material given in the circles before it, and rushing ahead before you've absorbed the lessons of one circle will make it harder for you to do anything with the lessons of the next. One of the standard mottoes of traditional occultism is worth remembering here: *festina lente*, which literally means "hurry slowly!" The more patience, perseverance, and hard work you apply to this material, the more you will get out of it.

---

[8] Many other churches do not do this, but the UGC has its own traditions.

CHAPTER TWO

The second circle

The work of the second circle has the same basic foundation as the material you have already covered in the first circle: the basic practices you learned in *The Way of the Golden Section*, the three exercises given in the previous section of this book, the visualization of the temple before you begin your meditation and the visualization of your guardian angel afterwards. The temple visualization changes in this circle, and in each of the circles to come; in addition, another practice is inserted into the second step of the energy-awakening exercise, just after the temple visualization and just before you massage the back of your head. The first step in awakening the palm centers for healing and blessing, the first of the Gnostic Lessons, and the first of the minor orders, the order of Cleric, also belong to this circle. We'll proceed through these one at a time.

Visualizing the temple: Phase two

The temple visualization in this circle builds on the one you practiced in the first circle. The landscape is the same as before, but there is an important change: the grass has been cleared away to reveal bare soil, and a design of stakes connected by ropes has been laid out on the ground to show the basic geometry of the temple to be. The diagram below shows the way the stakes and ropes are laid out. Your place is at the seat shown in the diagram.

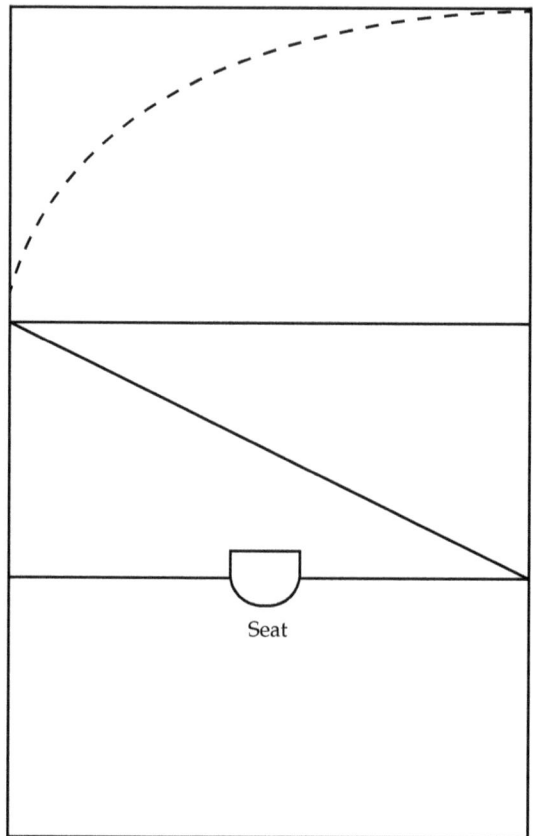

The solid lines are ropes, tied to stakes driven in at the corners. The dotted line is a mark on the ground made by swinging the left end of the diagonal line to form a Golden Rectangle.

Temple geometry 1

The design shown here sets out one of the standard ways to lay out a Golden Rectangle—that is, a rectangle in which the ratio of the long sides to the short sides is the Golden Section, or Φ. This rectangle provides the ground plan of your temple, and the line traced by the rope just ahead of you is the division between the two main parts of your temple: the naos or nave, which is the place where you will normally be seated, and the adytum or sanctuary, which is the place set aside for the manifestation of spiritual forces.[9] This division and its applications to the secret temple you are constructing will be discussed further as we proceed.

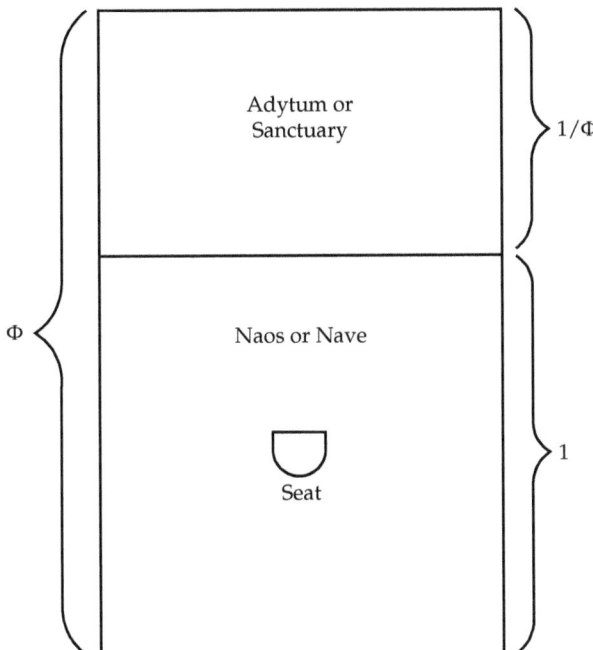

The ground plan of your temple, divided according to the Golden Section. "Naos" and "Adyton" are ancient Greek terms, "Nave" and "Sanctuary" their medieval English equivalents.

Temple design 1

During the time you spend on this circle, spend five minutes or so visualizing the scene described above. As you did with the first temple visualization, see and sense this scene as clearly as possible, and then release the imagery and proceed to the awakening of the first two of the seven vortices, as described below.

---

[9] The terms "naos" and "adytum" come from Pagan temple traditions, while the words "nave" and "sanctuary" are from the Christian tradition. You may use either set of terms; both will be used in this book.

The first two vortices

The seven vortices are activated during your preparation for meditation, between the temple visualization and rubbing the back of your head at the beginning of the energy-awakening exercise. In this and the following circles, you will learn to awaken the vortices one or two at a time. For this circle, the vortices you will work with are the knee vortices. These are located just behind the kneecap of each knee, in the space between the bones of the lower and upper leg.

Very few spiritual traditions make use of energy centers in the legs, and those that do mostly focus on a pair of centers in the sole of each foot. In India, however, the knee centers are known as the sutala chakras, and they play an important role in certain traditions of inner work. They are also central to certain branches of the Rosicrucian tradition, and the exercises to activate them that are presented in this book come from that latter source.

There are many ways to awaken the subtle centers of the body. The method that you will be using involves concentration and visualization, two of the most important tools of the occultist. Begin, once you have finished your temple visualization, by turning your attention to your knees. Feel them, and pay particular attention to the space right behind the kneecaps. Now imagine a star shining with bright white light in each of your knees, located in the space just described.

Both stars now begin turning clockwise. (Imagine that your meditation chair is resting on a gigantic clock face; the way the hands would move is "clockwise" for this purpose.) Your goal is to get them spinning clockwise as quickly as possible. They may be sluggish or resistant at first, but keep working at it. Breathe slowly and steadily in and out until you have taken seven breaths, spinning the stars in your knees all the while. Then release the imagery, and proceed to the rest of the energy-awakening exercise and from there to your meditation.

What is the point of visualizing the turning stars? The astral plane, as you have already learned, is the plane of imagination, dreams, and visionary experiences. You can influence it through concentration on images held in your mind's eye. Your astral body, which is of course part of the astral plane, is no exception to this rule. By concentrating on the image of rotating stars at certain specific points on our bodies, we exercise the astral body and increase its strength and flexibility. Since the astral body influences the etheric body, and the etheric body influences the material body, the effects of this practice will also gradually filter down the planes to give additional strength to your bodies of life energy and ordinary matter.

These effects on the material body are central to the work of these two vortices in a way that is not true of the remaining five. The knee vortices, in our work, are assigned to the material plane, and they provide a gentle stimulus to certain other energy centers also linked to the material plane. By awakening them in the method just explained, you will strengthen your ability to act on the material plane, and to bring your material body into closer harmony with the other levels of yourself.

Eventually you will be applying the same visualizations to all seven of the vortices, and activating the rest of your bodies. In the circles to come we will add more vortices one by one to this phase of the work, but for now concentrate on the knee vortices alone. Pay attention to any effects of the awakening of these vortices that you may notice, and record them in your practice journal.

Awakening the palm centers

The seven vortices and the solar plexus are the most important energy centers used in the Golden Section system for your own personal occult and spiritual development. Certain practical applications of the work, require the activation of two more centers, which are located at the base of each palm. If you look at one of your palms, you will find a low mound of flesh around the base of your thumb and another, smaller mound on the other side of the palm, just above your wrist. You will also find two or three "bracelet lines" where your palm joins your forearm. (If you have trouble seeing these, bend your palm slightly toward you). The palm center is at the base of the palm, between the two mounds and just above the bracelet lines closest to your palm.

The two palm centers have a wide range of uses in occult practice. In this circle you will begin learning how to awaken the palm centers. In the circles to come we will go on to explore some of the ways to empower them and work with them for the purposes of healing, blessing, and initiation. You may also find, once you have learned how to work with the centers, other ways to work with them. The goal of your training, after all, is not to lock you into some fixed set of practices, but to provide you with a toolkit you can use in many different ways in the quest for wisdom, revelation, and enlightenment.

Awakening the left palm

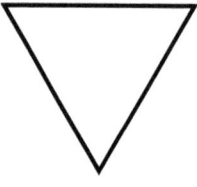

At this stage in your training, the process of awakening your palm centers should be made part of your daily practices. When you have finished the self-massage at the end of your daily meditation, draw a triangle on the palm of your left hand with the index finger of your right hand. Start the triangle at the base of your left palm just above the wrist. Trace the triangle clockwise from there to the base of your left index finger, across to the base of your left little finger, and back to the point of beginning. Imagine your finger drawing the triangle in a line of vivid blue light. This triangle, as in the Sphere of Protection ritual, represents the element of Water and the gate of Dŵr.

Then, with your right index finger, draw a clockwise circle on the palm of your left hand. The circle begins at the starting point of the triangle and goes up to the base of your fingers. Imagine your finger drawing the circle in a line of vivid green light. When the finger returns to the point where it began, draw a straight line from there up your wrist about as long as your palm is tall. This green circle with its descending line, as in the Sphere of Protection ritual, represents the element of Earth and the gate of Daear.

Awakening the right palm

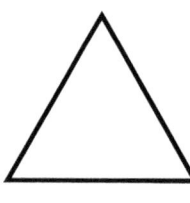

Now go to the other hand, and trace a triangle on the palm of your right hand with your left index finger. Start the triangle at a point just below the gap between your ring and middle fingers. Trace the triangle clockwise, down to the base of your thumb, straight across to the outside edge of your palm, and back to the point of beginning. Imagine your finger drawing this triangle in a line of vivid red light. This triangle, as in the Sphere of Protection ritual, represents the element of Fire and the gate of Ufel.

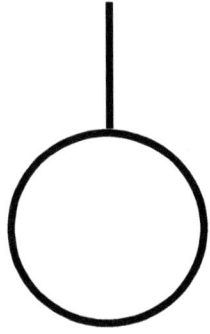

Next, still using your left index finger, draw a clockwise circle on the palm of your right hand, starting at the same point where you began the triangle and surrounding the entire palm. Imagine your finger drawing this circle in a line of vivid yellow light. When the finger returns to the point where it began, draw a straight line from there up between and to the tips of your second and third fingers. The yellow circle with its ascending line, as in the Sphere of Protection ritual, represents the element of Air and the gate of Awyr.

Joining the centers

At this point, when you have traced the symbols on your hands, bring your hands together with the energy center at the base of each palm pressed against the other. The fingers of the left hand should point forward, away from your body, with the palm facing right, while the fingers of the right hand should point upwards, with the palm facing left. The fingers may be held straight or allowed to curve gently, as you prefer. Hold them in this position while breathing slowly and evenly for a time, then rotate the fingers of the left hand to point upwards, separate the hands, and clap them together once, crisply and forcefully. This final action seals the energy and makes it possible for you to go about your day without leaking energy through your palm centers.

An important occult teaching is hidden in these simple gestures. The right hand, which is symbolically related to the solar current, is used to awaken the centers of the left hand, and the left hand, which is symbolically related to the telluric current, is used to awaken the centers of the right hand. Then both hands join to finish the process of activating each other. Each hand transmits energy to the other, and the energies are of opposite polarity but equal power.

Practice awakening the palm centers as described after your meditation each day. Later circles will build on this exercise.

The order of Cleric

The first of the minor orders of the Universal Gnostic Church, the order of Cleric, also belongs to this circle. Many people these days know the term "cleric" mostly through roleplaying games such as

Dungeons & Dragons™, in which clerics are a character class. If you want to think of the work of the minor orders as something like the process of becoming a first-level Cleric, that's fine, but remember that you are doing this work in the real world, not the world of roleplaying games![10]

The training of the Cleric is dedicated to the analysis of our physical bodies. Throughout these lessons, emphasis will be placed on heightening both your physical, emotional (psychic), and spiritual intuition; we hope also to impart to you, the seeker, useful techniques for harnessing and controlling your whole being to aid in the quest for spiritual enlightenment. We are not our mere material beings, we are more than creatures of matter—but we do have material bodies, and need to include them in the process of our inner development.

This is an important step in our spiritual evolution. It is important for us to realize that we are not our bodies, that we are more than our material bodies, but it is also important for us to realize that we aren't in material existence by accident. As Clerics, we remind ourselves we are spiritual beings and know we are temporarily inhabiting material bodies for good reason.

The order of Cleric is associated with the faculty of taste. Modern ways have taught us to ignore our subtle sense of taste and only rely on our gross sense of taste. This allows food vendors to pump us full of salt, white sugar and refined fats—all of which are bad for our health. Excess salt is implicated in a range of health problems, including heart disease. White sugar and refined fats are difficult for our bodies to process and are also implicated in a range of health problems. They taste good to our gross sense of taste but they are not good for us.

Fast food equates to "eat fast." Eating while working or "on the run" equates to "eat fast." Eating quickly is one way to bypass your subtle sense of taste. Eating a lot of salt, white sugar and refined fats is another. Fast food is a double whammy to your taste buds. It's also a double whammy to your intuitive maturation. We'll cover this later on in this lesson.

One way to slow down and treat our food and drink with the respect they deserve is to take up the practice of saying grace before each meal. Saying grace is a form of blessing, and the sacrament of blessing is the

---

[10] This has its advantages. Do you really want to have to fight owlbears or gelatinous cubes?

special privilege of the order of Cleric. This, too, will be covered later on in this lesson.

You are encouraged at this point to add prayer to your routine of practices. Prayer doesn't need to take forever and it doesn't need to be complicated. Just find time to stand, kneel or sit down and talk with the Divine. Relax and breathe deeply. Be yourself. The Divine knows who you are, and won't pay attention to anything but the real you anyway. Just talk with the Divine as you would talk with a wise and sympathetic elder.

There are many techniques of prayer which you can find discussed in books on the subject. Far more important than technique, however, is the recognition that prayer is a relationship. You are making contact with the Divine, who is everywhere and in everything, the unfailing source of all that is. In truth, you've never been out of contact with the Divine. What's happening now is that you're making the contact consciously, accepting and acknowledging what has been going on all along.

As a Cleric you are empowered to continue following your own spiritual path. Clerics are enjoined to remember that each of our spiritual paths is unique. Others may follow a similar path, but the path followed by each of us is unique to us. Spiritual paths may cross, as indeed they do as we grow spiritually, and what seemed correct yesterday may not be so today. This is part of the learning process we all go through as we spiritually mature.

Being a Cleric is being a student. It is our responsibility as Clerics to continue studying your spiritual path, and continually to determine the right and proper path for us as individuals. Clerics see the alb—the white robe that is the symbol of clerical standing in the Universal Gnostic Church—as a symbol for both the mastery of our material body and the rebirth or refining of our current material body into our future glorified spiritual body.

The sacrament of blessing

One of the rights and duties of the minor order of Cleric is the sacrament of blessing. This is a ritual for recognizing and enhancing the beneficial and nurturing aspects of the Divine within a person, place or thing. A blessing raises the vibration of the object or entity being blessed if and only if such raising of vibration is acceptable to that being blessed.

Blessings are commonly used to bless food and drink, rooms, homes, objects that appeal to the one doing the blessing and other people, but anything, any place and any time may be blessed. It is always appropriate to ask for consent before giving a blessing, but it is also appropriate to give a blessing when consent is not an option: for example, when a person is unconscious as a result of an injury, or for other beings and things that cannot communicate their consent to you.

As we travel a spiritual path, our awareness of non-physical entities becomes more and more acute. Some of these entities are earthbound for one reason or another. Blessing them is one thing we can do to help them become more and more aware of their own spiritual path.

The following guidelines may be used for blessings:

1. Invoke the Divine (example: "Dear Creator …")
2. Ask for a blessing (example: "please send a blessing to …")
3. Give the name of the person, place or thing to be blessed
4. Describe any benefit of this blessing (example: "and lift their burden …")
5. Touch the person, animal or object to be blessed (optional)
6. Give thanks (example: "Thank you, Creator.")
7. Close (Examples: "Amen, So Be It, And it is so.")

If you prefer a simpler form, simply say the words "bless you," or "I ask the Divine to bless you" or use some other words of your choice. You may also use the standard form, "In the name of (deity), I bless you."

Giving a blessing to others is one way to advance your own spiritual life, because by lifting up others you also lift up yourself. Any blessing you send to others also comes back to you. Some spiritual teachers suggest that there's an 80–20 rule which says 80% of the good you give to others accrues to them and 20% to you. Others suggest instead that there's a 90–10 rule which means you accrue 10% of the good you give to others. But when you give evil to others, according to these same spiritual teachers, you accrue either 80% or 90% of the evil to yourself. Blessings are a better choice.

Make it a habit to bless someone or something every day. The more you bless, the more blessed the world becomes and the more you will be blessed.

Chewing, nutrition, and exercise

As strange as it may sound, one of the ways to increase your intuitive abilities is to chew your food. The more aware you become of the taste of the things you put into your mouth, the more your subtle energies are able to communicate with you. By becoming more aware of the tastes of different things, the more aware your mind becomes of everything, and this enhances your psychic and intuitive abilities.

Have you ever tasted something and the thing you tasted wasn't there? If you haven't already experienced this phenomenon, you will. If you have, welcome to the world of expanding intuition. If not, you can expect to taste things that aren't (physically) there as you continue your spiritual development. You may just be sitting there thinking of nothing in particular or you may be hard at work when you taste something, something you haven't put in your mouth. That taste is your intuitive mind telling you something. Pay attention. It may be a reminder to eat or drink something, it may be a memory, it may be your imagination, or may be a message from beyond. Be open to any possibility.

The sense of taste is enhanced by chewing your food. It's the act of breaking your food into small pieces that releases the essences picked up by our taste buds. When we gulp down food we don't taste it, we don't digest it well, we don't obtain full nutritional value from our food and we overtax our digestive system.

Fully tasting your food requires thoroughly chewing your food. According to medical studies, the human digestive system is designed to receive fully pulverized, saliva-drenched food. It is not designed to handle the big chunks of food the vast majority of modern people gobble down and dump into their stomachs. To fully masticate your food requires between 30 to 100 chewing and grinding actions by your teeth. Learn to chew your food completely and slowly. Learn to enjoy the taste of your food. Make this your priority during this period of study as you become a Cleric.

Tasting your food is part of the process of coming to terms with your physical body. Eating a balanced diet is the second part of that process. You'll find as you advance on your spiritual path that you'll eat less food at meals and in-between meals: your eating habits will become more moderate. This is because overeating is a nervous habit that you overcome as you become more peaceful. Traveling a spiritual path brings you more peace and less anger with life in general and yourself specifically. It also decreases your levels of fear and sadness.

Our modern sources of food often do not contain the nutritional values they did 50 or 100 years ago. As we travel our spiritual path and become more and more intuitive, it becomes increasingly important for us to have not only a balanced diet but a nourishing one as well. Our immune systems need to be fortified. You may find that a diet rich in nourishing foods is all you need, or you may find that you need vitamin and mineral supplements in order to feel your best.

While studying to become a Cleric, review your own nutritional needs and decide if you need any antioxidants or vitamins added to your daily nutritional program. Make an effort to study your personal nutritional needs. Try changing your diet if your circumstances permit that. Be careful, however, not to get caught up in new-diet-itis! It so happens that most people feel better and have more energy if they change their diet, no matter what the new diet might be.

One person made media headlines a few years ago by going on a diet consisting solely of fast food from chain restaurants. He felt better and had more energy. Another got in the news by eating only potatoes. He also felt better and had more energy—for a while. In most people, new-diet-itis wears off in three to six months. That's what drives diet fads: each new diet seems to work wonders—for a while.

It's healthier and less stressful to simply work out a diet that keeps you healthy and happy, and stick to that. One very useful tool for this purpose is a food diary. To keep a food diary, all you have to do is note down each day what you ate, and then at the end of the day, how you felt, how energetic you were, and whether you had any symptoms of illness. That's a quick way to find out if you have food sensitivities—if you feel really ill the next day every time you eat something, for example, try leaving it out of your diet for a month and see what that does for your health—but it also gives you a broader guide to what makes you more or less healthy. Try it and see.

While you're doing this, pay attention to how much exercise your body needs. Some people get more exercise than they need, while many more get less. Exercise doesn't have to involve going to the gym or running laps. There are many forms of exercise, and there is also the habit of doing things with your muscles rather than with machines—walking instead of driving or taking transit, for example. If you already have an exercise routine that satisfies you, that's good. If not, try out some new options and see how they work for you.

Ceremony of commitment for a Cleric

Once you have put at least a month into the work outlined above you will have completed the traditional requirements to become a Cleric in the Universal Gnostic Church. This title confers no special privilege upon you. It doesn't give you the right to tell other people what to do, or for that matter to preen yourself on your supposedly superior spiritual status. It simply reflects a commitment on your part to enter into a relationship with the Divine and to bless the world around you.

The ceremony is a way of honoring your acceptance of the work before you. It's a ceremony of commitment, which affirms that you have begun to understand what it means to be a Cleric and are willing to accept whatever the Divine may ask you to do. In order to perform this ritual, you will need certain things.

First, you will need holy water and a small amount of holy oil; instructions for preparing these are given at the end of this circle. You will also need a small pair of sharp scissors. In addition, you will need the standard gear you use to open a lodge of the Golden Section Fellowship. You may wish to write out in advance the prayers and vow discussed below, and have them in a convenient place as well. For the ritual, set aside an hour or so of uninterrupted time, and be sure that you will have privacy.

The ritual itself consists of eight steps.

First, open a lodge of the Golden Section Fellowship in the usual form. Make sure the holy water, holy oil, scissors, and written prayers and vow (if you are using these) are close to the altar of your lodge.

Second, say a prayer in which you thank the Divine, calling on whatever name or names you prefer, for all the gifts bestowed upon you. Ask for Divine blessings upon the lodge and yourself. Ask the Divine to be present and to accept you as a Cleric. You may use a spontaneous prayer, or write out a prayer in advance.

Third, say aloud a vow to the Divine to uphold the office of Cleric and to serve as a Cleric to the best of your ability, and then ask the Divine to assist you in keeping and fulfilling these vows. This also may be spontaneous, or written out in advance.

Fourth, cut a few strands of your hair. This symbolizes the tonsure, the shaving of a portion of the head that is used to mark entrance into the clergy in several faiths. By doing this you are symbolically offering yourself to the Divine.[11]

Fifth, purify yourself with holy water. This is done by dipping your fingertips into the water and using them to moisten your eyelids, your ears, your nostrils, and your lips with holy water. Dip your fingers into the water between each of these. While purifying yourself, say something like this: "I purify my senses so that I will be able to perceive the spiritual realms of existence, so help me (name of the Divine being used)."

Sixth, anoint yourself with holy oil on your third eye, which is above the bridge of your nose in the center of your forehead just above the eye ridge. In anointing yourself, say something like this: "I anoint myself to perform all the duties of a Cleric, so help me (name of the Divine being used)."

Seventh, say a prayer of thanksgiving, thanking the Divine for the blessings that have been conferred on you. Then take your seat and meditate for a time on the experience of the ceremony.

Eighth, close your lodge in the usual way.

Please note that the point of this ritual is not to impress anybody, including yourself. You gain no special status nor any authority over other people by becoming a Cleric. The point of the ceremony is to humbly and sincerely communicate with the Divine, take your vow, and bless the work the Divine will hereafter ask of you. Having completed the ceremony you are a Cleric. You are now ready to go forth and do such work as the Divine asks of you.

Holy water and holy oil

You will need these for your ceremony of commitment, and for other ceremonies and practices to come. They are simple to make. Holy water is simply water that has had a few grains of blessed salt dropped into it. Holy oil is simply olive oil that has been blessed.

To make holy water, place a few grains of salt on anything non-metallic—a wooden spoon, for example, or a small piece of paper.

---

[11] Some religious traditions specifically forbid this. If your beliefs will not permit you to do this, omit this step.

Bless the salt, following the instructions given earlier for the sacrament of blessing, and then put it in the water, blessing the water as you do so.

To make holy oil, simply put a small amount of pure olive oil in a bottle or other container and bless it, using the instructions given earlier. If you like, you can mix in a small amount of any essential oil you wish, but this is not required.

Completing the second circle

Plan on devoting at least one month to learning and practicing the work of this circle. Before you go on to the next circle, review all the material assigned to the second circle and be sure you understand it and have practiced it correctly. Remember that you can always take more time to complete the work if you wish. When you are ready, proceed to the third circle.

CHAPTER THREE

The third circle

The work of the third circle is once again based on the material you have already covered in the first two circles: the basic practices you learned in *The Way of the Golden Section*, the three exercises given in the previous section of this book, the visualization of the temple before you begin your meditation and the visualization of your guardian angel afterwards. At this stage of the work, the temple visualization changes again, and you will add another vortex into the second step of your preparation for meditation each day, just after the temple visualization and just before you massage the back of your head. The second stage in awakening the palm centers for healing and blessing, the second of the Gnostic Lessons, and the second of the minor orders, the order of Doorkeeper, also belong to this circle. As before, we'll proceed through these one at a time.

Visualizing the temple: Phase three

The temple visualization in this circle builds on the first two visualizations you have already done. The surrounding landscape is the same, and you are still seated in the same place on your wooden chair, but the ropes and stakes have been replaced by a foundation. The workmen have dug trenches where the outer rectangle of ropes ran, laid down a first course of squared stone blocks in the trenches, and packed the earth back in around the sides of the stone blocks. Another course of stone blocks has been laid down on the line dividing the naos or nave from the adytum or sanctuary, as shown in the previous circle. The temple has therefore begun its journey from the abstract into a manifest reality in the worlds of your imagination.

During the time you spend on this circle, spend five minutes or so visualizing the scene described above. As you did with the first two temple visualizations, see and sense this scene as clearly as possible, and then release the imagery and proceed to the awakening of the first three of the seven vortices, as described below.

The third vortex

In this stage of the work you will add a third vortex to the two you are already activating: the genital vortex, which is located just above and behind the base of the penis or clitoris. This does not mean that this vortex is all about sex! The genital region is the great center of etheric life in the body, and when this vortex is activated it energizes, awakens, and directs the etheric body. If your sex life has been stifled or drained of force by psychological or medical issues, work with this vortex will tend to help revive it, but if your sexuality has been overactive, work with this vortex will tend to calm it down and recirculate the energies to other purposes. Here as always in our work, equilibrium is the keynote.

In this stage of the work, you will start by visualizing the two knee vortices spinning, but you will do this for three breaths only, rather than the seven breaths you used in the first circle. Then visualize a star at the location of your genital vortex. Begin spinning that in a clockwise direction, the same direction as the knee vortices. Breathe in and out while visualizing the spinning star, until you have taken seven slow, steady breaths. Then release the imagery you have built up and go on to the rest of the energy-awakening exercise.

Charging the palm centers

By the time you begin the work of this circle you will have done the exercise to awaken your palm centers daily for a month or more. During the time you spend on this circle, you will continue that exercise, but you will also perform an exercise to charge your palm centers by linking them to the elemental energies corresponding to them. This is done using the same methods you used for scrying in *The Way of the Four Elements*. Your task in the third circle is to do this once with each of the elements in the same order you awaken the centers—Water, Earth, Fire, and Air—using Water and Earth to charge the center in your left Palm and Fire and Air to charge the center in your right palm. Do each of these chargings as a separate working.

Charging with the element of Water

Put a chair in the West of your working space, facing East. Then perform the Sphere of Protection ritual to clear and cleanse the space for your working. Once you have finished the Sphere of Protection, go to the eastern side of your working space and face West, toward the chair and the symbolic direction of the element of Water. Trace the downward-pointing triangle of Water with the first two fingers of your right hand, beginning at the bottom point and going clockwise from there. As you trace it, imagine yourself drawing the triangle in a line of brilliant blue light. Then point to the center of the triangle and say:

"In the name of the Eternal Spiritual Sun" (or of the deity you pray to), "may a portal be opened for me into the realm of elemental Water. May I be welcomed by the spirits and powers of Water, that I may charge my left palm center with Water."

Imagine the triangle expanding until it is large enough for you to step through. Wait until you feel a sense that you are welcome to step through the portal, or until you hear in your imagination a voice telling you to enter. Step through the triangle, turn around, and sit down in the chair. Once you do so, imagine the triangle shrinking to a point and going far away, leaving you wholly within the realm of elemental Water.

While working through *The Way of the Four Elements* you learned how to attune yourself with the elements in scrying. Do the same thing this time by visualizing yourself surrounded by an ocean of clear blue light, and then allowing this to transform in your imagination to an ocean of water. Feel the water moving around you and through you.

Next, trace the blue triangle of Water on your left palm with the index finger of your right hand. Do not trace the other symbols at this time—just the triangle of Water. When you are ready, raise your left hand, feeling the ocean of water around it. In your own words, ask the element of Water to charge the palm center in your left hand, and feel the energies of water flowing into and out of the energy center in the base of your left palm, charging and empowering it. Maintain this for seven slow even breaths. Then thank the powers of Water for their help.

At this point ask for permission to leave the realm of elemental Water. When you feel the answer, or hear an imagined voice telling you that you may leave, get up from the chair, step through the portal, go to the eastern side of your working space, and turn to face the portal. Imagine the triangle returning to the size you originally drew in the air. Thank the powers of Water for the help you have received, and then trace the triangle again with the first two fingers of your right hand. Start from the lowest point again, but go counterclockwise, and as your fingers move along the line of blue light, see them erasing the line. When you are finished, the triangle is completely gone. Clap your hands together to seal the energy center in your palm and finish the working.

Charging with the other elements

This is done in exactly the same way as the element of Water, except that you place the chair facing the direction of the element, you trace the emblem of the element in the air and also on your hand, you invoke the element in question, and you charge your palm center with the energy of another element rather than Water energy. Review the instructions for scrying in *The Way of the Four Elements* if you have any questions about how these workings are done. Again, you will be doing each of the elemental chargings as a separate working, and you will do them in the following order—Water, Earth, Fire, and Air—the same order in which you trace the elemental emblems when you awaken the palm centers.

Meanwhile, continue the practice of awakening your palm centers each day after your daily meditation. You may begin to notice a sense of energy present in your hands as you proceed with this work, and your hands may also become more sensitive to etheric and astral forces. This is known as clairtangence; it is to the sense of touch what clairvoyance is to the sense of sight, and it has many useful applications in occult work.

The order of Doorkeeper

The training of the Doorkeeper is dedicated to the analysis of our emotional life, assigned to the soul or psyche by some classical Gnostics. Throughout the course of this lesson, emphasis will be placed on heightening both your physical, emotional (psychic), and spiritual intuition; we hope also to impart to you, the seeker, useful techniques for harnessing and controlling your emotions to aid in the quest for spiritual enlightenment. We are not our mere material beings, we are more than creatures of matter. We also possess an emotional self.

This recognition is an important step in our spiritual evolution. The realization that we are more than our physical bodies is but the first step. The second, and often more difficult step, is to also realize that we are more than our emotional lives. It is easy to become blinded by our emotional state of the moment, to forget who we really are. As Doorkeepers, we remind ourselves that we are spiritual beings, and we come to know that we are more than just our body and the emotions we experience.

In ancient times the doorkeeper of a church or temple had important duties. He was expected to guard the door during sacred rituals, preventing any interruption of the work, and he was also responsible for welcoming honored guests and recognizing the spiritual standing of anyone who approached the temple or church door. In the same way, you must learn to guard the doors of your mind, closing those doors to interruptions when those are inappropriate, welcoming insights and inspirations from the Divine, and recognizing the value of thoughts and feelings that present themselves.

The order of Doorkeeper is associated with the faculty of smell. We need to learn to stop and smell the roses for it is through smelling the roses we begin to fathom the truth that we are more than the emotions we feel. A whole new world opens up to us as our sense of smell rises into the subtle realms. Fragrances take on more meaning for us as we learn to appreciate both their delight and their higher vibrations.

While serving as a Doorkeeper, you are expected to examine your emotional health and address any weaknesses you find. One way to begin this work is to reflect on the feelings of shame, blame, and guilt you feel concerning events in your past and present. The practice of journaling discussed in *The Way of the Golden Section* is a good way to do this. Try this exercise: at the top of a page in your journaling notebook, write down a simple statement about a feeling you have about yourself, such as "I feel ashamed about (some event in my past)." Then write down whatever comes to mind in response to that statement. No matter how silly, hurtful, or wrong the thought may be, write it down. Get it on paper. You can then ask questions—for example, "Why do I still feel this way?"—and once again write down everything that comes to mind in response. This is a very effective way to let your subjective mind express and release hurts it still carries from events in your past.

Most of our emotional problems are rooted in feelings of inadequacy, inferiority, unworthiness, helplessness, hopelessness, and ineffectiveness. These feelings are always more or less inaccurate—though it is important not to forget that the opposite of one bad idea is another bad idea, and swing from feelings of inadequacy to feelings of egotistic self-glorification. There is a middle ground between these two states, a place of calm recognition of our own strengths and weaknesses. As Doorkeepers, we can open the doors that will allow us to pass into that middle ground.

We all function as Doorkeepers in our lives. We must sometimes aid other people in working through their own negative emotions and experiences. We function as Doorkeepers for these individuals and allow them to step over the threshold to continue their journeys. We open the door or gate for them and they can enter into a new phase of their spiritual path. Likewise, other people are keeping the door closed to us until we work through our own issues. Then the door opens and we may proceed.

On an esoteric level we function in a similar manner. None may pass through the door we guard until he or she resolves her or his issues with us. The password required is the message to be delivered, a request for acceptance or forgiveness, or the issue to be settled between us. Opening the door is a sign we received the message and we forgive this person or the issue has been settled.

Your work as a Cleric

You do not cease to be a Cleric when you begin training as a Doorkeeper. More generally, each minor order you receive adds to the previous order, rather than replacing it. As a Cleric, you will benefit by continuing the practice of daily prayer, and performing the sacrament of blessing as often as you have an opportunity. You will also benefit by continuing the practices involving food and exercise set out in the previous lesson. Make these practices a regular part of your daily life and you will reap their benefits.

Your work with the palm centers may already be having a positive effect on your ability to bless. During the work of this and the following circles, whenever you can do this without attracting attention, extend your hands toward whatever you are blessing and visualize positive spiritual energies radiating from your palm centers to enhance the blessing. This practice will be amplified by more focused methods in later circles.

The sacrament of naming

Most Christian churches practice the sacrament of baptism for infants. The Universal Gnostic Church does not practice infant baptism because it places a high value on the autonomy and freedom of the individual soul. Only when a person has reached the age where he or she can make a thoughtful decision to make a personal commitment to a given faith is baptism appropriate.

However, it is entirely appropriate to formally name and bless an infant, and to commend the infant to the protection of the Divine. In the Universal Gnostic Church we confer a name and blessing to infants with the sacrament of naming. The same sacrament may also be conferred on people of any age who wish to take a new name, or to mark an interior change of being, thinking, feeling, doing, or intending or the start of something new. This is one of the duties of the Doorkeeper, who opens the door to a new name and new life through the sacrament of naming.

Once you have completed the requirements for this minor order and become a Doorkeeper, you have the right and duty to perform the sacrament of naming for other people under the auspices of the Universal Gnostic Church. Whenever you exercise this function, keep a record of it. In this record include the name of the person and the circumstances in which the sacrament was requested and carried out.

The ceremony of naming is quite simple. Prepare a small quantity of holy water in advance. Find out from the person to be named, or the parents or guardians of an infant, what name will be conferred and what name, if any, will be used to invoke the Divine; this is theirs to decide and not yours. Pray, silently or aloud, asking the Divine to bless the person you are about to name. Then pour a small amount of holy water on the head of the person being named and say, "I name you (name) in the presence of (deity). May the blessing and the protection of (deity) be with you all the days of your life." If the naming ceremony is for an adult, and the name is being taken for some specific purpose, you may add: "… for the purpose of (name the purpose)." Follow with a prayer of thanksgiving, silent or aloud.

Smell and intuition

The sense of smell is the first that seems to manifest itself as we work our way through the Gnostic Lessons. You may already be aware you smell things more often and intensely since starting your studies.

This process of opening up your psychic sense of smell—clairflairance, to give it its proper name—will continue as you work your way through the Gnostic Lessons. You can quicken this development by consciously paying attention to the things you smell on a day-to-day basis. Being more aware of smells in both the physical and psychic worlds is a spiritual practice that helps the student raise his or her vibration to higher levels.

"Take time to smell the roses" is a common way of telling others to slow down and pay attention to life. It's also good advice for the spiritual traveler. As we slow down we become more peaceful and calm. In this state our sense of smell is heightened. Paying attention to the things we smell in this state increases our ability to use our sense of smell and it increases our spiritual vibration.

A good practice is to stop doing whatever we're doing several times a day. Relax and breathe deeply for a few seconds. Then pay attention to the smells around us. This can be done while sitting, standing, walking or resting. It doesn't matter when, where or how we "stop to smell the roses." What matters is that we consciously take the time to do so.

As you persist in this practice you'll start to smell things you don't remember ever smelling before. This is natural. As you pay attention to any of your senses, that sense will perform better for you. Paying attention to anything increases our awareness of the object of our attention. Paying attention to our sense of smell increases our awareness of the myriad smells around us.

As you pay attention, you become more aware. You'll also start to smell things that aren't physically there. For example, in the dead of winter without a flower in sight, you may experience the smell of roses.

This impossible situation of smelling things that aren't actually there may confuse and concern you in the beginning. Don't worry, this is merely a sign you're developing your clairflairance. Just enjoy the moment.

The first psychic smells will probably be the result of spiritual beings bringing you these things in the astral world. If you smell roses, somebody on the other side is bringing you roses. If you smell a barnyard, somebody on the other side is reminding you of something. Whatever psychic smells you experience have a meaning and a message. If you want to develop your psychic senses, pay attention to these things and look for both the message and the meaning.

If you pay attention to your sense of smell you'll experience psychic smelling for yourself. Once you experience smelling something that isn't there you'll naturally shift your attention to looking attentively for somebody to approach your door. It's natural. It's part of growing spiritually. It's part of your duty as a Doorkeeper.

Practice being aware of your sense of smell. Expect clairflairant experiences and look for the person or persons coming to your gate or door. Be aware. Be prepared. Be ready to accept whatever the other person brings into your life and open the door for that person.

Opening the door or gate for others means that you give them the thing they need to continue their spiritual journey. This may be advice or counsel but it could also be acceptance, forgiveness and love. As soon as you give whatever it is the other person needs from you, he or she will continue on his or her spiritual journey and so will you. Until you give the other person whatever it is he or she needs from you that person may continue to need something from you. Needy people can be a thorn in your side.

Anytime you have needy people in your life, your best approach is to relax, breathe deeply and become aware. In this state, ask the Divine to help you open the door for this needy person or these needy people. Pay attention. Be receptive. Accept whatever it is the other person or persons bring to you. Open the door.

Other senses will also become active in this way. As you advance through the Gnostic Lessons all your senses of smell, taste, touch, hearing and sight will open psychically. When you perceive something out of the ordinary with any of these senses, pay attention as you're probably being asked to serve your duty as a Doorkeeper. Once you become attuned as a Doorkeeper, your duty will include being a Doorkeeper for the rest of your life. Actually, you always had and always will have that duty, you're just more aware of that fact when you complete your attunement as a Doorkeeper.

Ceremony of commitment for a Doorkeeper

Once you have put at least a month into the work outlined above you will have completed the traditional requirements to become a Doorkeeper in the Universal Gnostic Church. This title confers no special privilege upon you. It doesn't give you the right to tell other people what to do, or to preen yourself on your supposedly superior spiritual status. It simply reflects a commitment on your part to enter into a relationship with the Divine and to bless the world around you. (Yes, these same cautions were included in the first Gnostic Lesson, before the instructions for becoming a Cleric, and they are repeated for every one of the minor orders. The mistaken notion that clergy can claim unearned status and tell other people what to do is so deeply rooted in our culture that multiple reminders are often needed to shake it loose.)

The ceremony is a way of honoring your acceptance of the work before you. It's a ceremony of commitment, which affirms that you understand what it means to be a Doorkeeper and accept whatever the Divine may ask you to do. In order to perform this ritual, you will need the same items you used in your Cleric ceremony of commitment, except the scissors.

The ritual itself consists of seven steps.

First, open a lodge of the Golden Section Fellowship in the usual form. Make sure the holy water, holy oil, and written prayers and vow (if you are using these) are close to the altar of your lodge.

Second, say a prayer in which you thank the Divine, using whatever name you prefer, for all the gifts bestowed upon you. Ask for Divine blessings upon the lodge and yourself. Ask the Divine to be present and to accept you as a Doorkeeper. You may use a spontaneous prayer, or write out a prayer in advance.

Third, vow to the Divine to uphold the office of Doorkeeper and to serve as a Doorkeeper to the best of your ability; and then ask the Divine to assist you in keeping and fulfilling these vows. This also may be spontaneous, or written out in advance.

Fourth, purify yourself with holy water. This is done by dipping your fingertips into the water and using them to moisten your eyelids, your ears, your nostrils, and your lips with holy water. Dip your fingers into the water between each of these. While purifying yourself, say something like this: "I purify my senses so that I will be able to perceive the spiritual realms of existence, so help me (name of the Divine being used)."

Fifth, anoint yourself with holy oil at the base of each palm, just past the wrist. In anointing yourself, say something like: "I anoint myself to perform all the duties of a Doorkeeper, so help me (name of the Divine being used)."

Sixth, say a prayer of thanksgiving, thanking the Divine for the blessings that have been conferred on you. Then take your seat and meditate for a time on the experience of the ceremony.

Seventh, close your lodge in the usual way.

Please note—and again, this point has been made already but it will be made again and again as you proceed—that the point of this ritual is not to impress anybody, including yourself. You gain no special status nor any authority over other people by becoming a Doorkeeper. The point of the ceremony is to humbly and sincerely communicate with the Divine, take your vow, and bless the work the Divine will hereafter ask of you. Having completed the ceremony you are a Doorkeeper. You are now ready to go forth and do such work as the Divine asks of you.

Completing the third circle

Plan on devoting at least one month to learning and practicing the work of this circle. Before you go on to the next circle, review all the material assigned to the third circle and be sure you understand it and have practiced it correctly. Remember that you can always take more time to complete the work if you wish. When you are ready, proceed to the fourth circle.

CHAPTER FOUR

The fourth circle

The work of the fourth circle has the same basis as the material you have already covered in the first three circles. The basic practices you learned in *The Way of the Golden Section*, the three exercises given in the previous section of this book, the visualization of the temple before you begin your meditation and the visualization of your guardian angel afterwards, are as important here as before. Once again, the temple visualization changes, and you will add a fourth vortex into the second step of the energy-awakening exercise, after the temple visualization and just before you massage the back of your head. The third stage in awakening the palm centers for healing and blessing, the third of the Gnostic Lessons and the third of the minor orders, the order of Reader, also belong to this circle. Again, we'll proceed through these one at a time.

Visualizing the temple: Phase four

The workers have been busy, and now the walls and floor of your temple have been put in place. The walls are made of neatly squared and smoothed blocks of stone in even rows, rising up to a height equal to the width of your temple. There are three tall openings for windows in the walls on your left and right, a doorway behind you, and a circular opening for a window high up in the wall ahead of you. All these are open to the air, since the windows and door have not yet been made by the craft workers, and of course the ceiling and roof have not yet been built.

The floor is covered with broad flat paving stones, also well squared and smoothed. Where the naos or nave gives way to the adytum or sanctuary, the floor rises up a single step. The temple at this stage looks roughly like the diagram below.

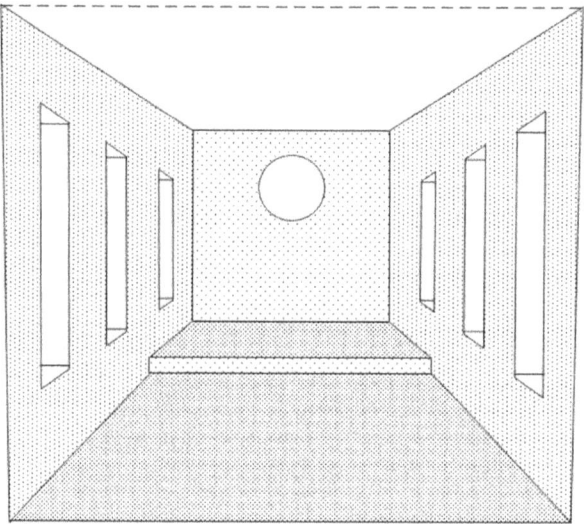

Temple design 2

During the time you spend on this circle, spend five minutes or so visualizing the scene described above. As you did with the earlier temple visualizations, see and sense this scene as clearly as possible, and then release the imagery and proceed to the awakening of the first four of the seven vortices, as described below.

The fourth vortex

The fourth vortex we will be working with is located inside the right side of the torso in the region of the liver, just below the ribcage in line with your right nipple. Of the seven vortices, this is the one most closely related to the astral body. Traditional occult lore has it that there are three seed atoms that form the starting point of your material, etheric, and astral bodies; the material seed atom is located in the heart, the etheric seed atom is in the spleen, and the astral seed atom is in the liver. These seed atoms thus form a triangle around the solar plexus.

The astral body extends out beyond the limits of the material body to form the aura. By awakening the fourth vortex, your aura is strengthened and energized. This makes it easier for you to throw off unwanted mental and emotional influences so you can follow your own path with less interference from others. This vortex also strengthens your psychic senses and increases your ability to work with your imagination. As you work with this vortex, you may find your dream life becoming more active, and any creative talents or interests you have are likely to be stirred up.

In this fourth stage of the work, you will start by visualizing the two knee vortices spinning, giving them three breaths each, and then proceed to visualize the genital vortex spinning, again for three breaths. Then visualize a star at the location of your liver vortex. Begin spinning that in a clockwise direction, the same direction as the other vortices. Breathe in and out while visualizing the spinning star, until you have taken seven slow, steady breaths. Then release the imagery and go on to the rest of the energy-awakening exercise.

The palm centers and the two currents

At this point you have been practicing the awakening of the palm centers for at least two months and have charged your palm centers once with each of the four elements. During the work of this circle, you should continue the daily practice of awakening the palm centers, and you should do one more set of charging the palm centers with the four elements, in the way explained in the previous circle. A third stage of the practice needs to be added at this point, however, before you can use your palm centers for healing and blessing with full effect.

The solar and telluric currents, the two great flows of magical force in the world of our experience, have many applications in occult practice. You learned already, when you took up the initiate's version of the Sphere of Protection, how to invoke the two currents into yourself, combine them to make the lunar current, and use this latter current to activate the solar plexus and pineal centers in the body. Later in this book you will learn and practice a ritual that calls on the two great currents to send positive energies throughout the area where you live, and you will also learn how to use the two currents in the work of initiation. The two currents can also be brought into the work of healing and blessing using the palm centers, and this is one of the subjects for you to study and practice in this circle.

This stage of the work follows on the awakening of your palm centers and so should be done each day after your meditation. Start by activating your palm centers in the way you have been taught, by tracing the symbols of Water and Earth on your left hand and the symbols of Fire and Air on your right hand. Place your hands together in front of your chest as you have been taught, with the bases of your palms joined. The slight hollow at the base of each hand marks the point at which an energy channel running along the center of your arm reaches the surface of your hand on the palm side, and spreads out through the palms and fingers. By joining the two hands together as described in an earlier circle, with the fingers of the left hand pointing forward and those of the right hand pointing up, these two energy centers are brought into close contact, completing a circuit that can then be used to direct the solar and telluric currents through your body.

This circuit is awakened by a pattern of imagery synchronized with your breath. As you breathe in, draw down a stream of the solar current from high above you. Visualize it as a stream of warm golden light, and feel it flowing like water. Bring it in through the top of your head, and down the midline of your body to the level of your heart, and then let it flow out to the right shoulder, through the right arm to the right hand, and through the joined energy centers into your left hand. It then continues around through the left arm and shoulder, angles down to meet the midline of the body again at the solar plexus, and descends through your legs in two streams to descend deep into the earth.

As you breathe out, visualize the telluric current following the same course in the opposite direction; visualize it as a stream of cool green light, the color of sunlight through leaves, and feel it flowing like water. It rises through the soles of your feet and goes up your legs to join into a single current just above your genitals, and then flows up the midline of your body to the solar plexus. There it flows left to your left shoulder and out through your left arm, through the joined energy centers, up your right arm to your right shoulder, from there back to the midline of your body at your heart, and up from there to the crown of your head and through it into the heavens.

Do this for three cycles of breath, so you have brought the solar current down while breathing in and the telluric current up while breathing out three times each. Later on, if you wish, you can increase this to nine cycles. When you are finished, bring your palms together, pivot them to a parallel position, and clap your hands together once as you have been taught, to seal the palm centers and keep the healing energy from leaking out.

The first few times you work your way through the process just described, you may find it interesting to test the energy flow between the palms. To do this, once you have completed the three breaths, but before you clap the hands together, draw your hands slowly apart and turn them so that the fingertips are pointing in the same direction. When they are a foot or so apart, pause, and imagine the energy still flowing from one to the other, the solar current from right to left and the telluric current from left to right. After a minute or so, begin moving your palms slowly toward one another and then away again. The total distance each hand moves should be no more than an inch or two. You may be surprised by the sensations you feel in your palms.

The order of Reader

The training of the Reader is dedicated to the analysis of your mental life, and to the sense of sight. As we become more mentally aware of who we really are, we gain insight into what makes us tick, what drives us to do what we do. This insight leads us to search deeper within ourselves. There we discover peace, love, and light—the peace which passeth understanding, the love of the Divine and all that is, and the light, which is the Light of the World and the light which is us.

We use our sense of sight to read the word of man and the Word of the Divine. We use it to see the world of man and the World of the Divine. As we refine our sight, we begin to see what is really there. We see the love of the Divine in everything, the rocks and mountains, the plants and flowers, the birds and animals, mankind and life. We see the light behind the thing. We begin to see this world as the spiritual world it is.

The process of opening and developing your third eye is part of the work you will do while serving as a Doorkeeper and learning to become a Reader. The third eye is part of your subtle body. It is located roughly where, in your physical body, the base of your nose meets your forehead—not far, in other words, from your pituitary gland. The opening of the third eye is a gradual process, beginning with a dim sense of "something present" and developing from there.

A certain part of your spiritual growth depends upon your being able to perceive and work in the astral world. Until your third eye opens you're basically blind in the astral. Don't let that bother you. As you practice the techniques you have already learned, your third eye will open, and once you begin working with the pituitary vortex in a later circle, your third eye will open more quickly than you might expect.

You have already learned that you are more than your material body, and that you are more than your emotions. Now you must learn that you are more than your ideas and thoughts. Many people identify themselves with their ideas and thoughts, and so the fear that they might be wrong about something cripples their ability to deal with life. We're all wrong about many things, all the time. As children of the Divine we still have much to learn about the universe and about ourselves, and that means that right now we're still wrong about a lot of things. Get used to it. We have all eternity to learn and grow into the truth that will set us free.

In ancient times just as in the present, the Reader of a church or temple has always had an important place. It was his work to read the sacred narratives aloud, so that others present were instructed and inspired. In the same way, you must learn to communicate the wisdom teachings of the world to yourself and to others through study, reading, and most important, through the way you live your life. Teaching by example is always the most effective approach to education.

The Office of Reader is associated with the faculty of sight. As a Reader it is your task to see clearly what is written, whether in books, or in the faces or hearts of other people, or in the Unseen. While serving as Readers, you are expected to thoroughly examine your thinking and address any weaknesses you find. None of us can know everything there is to be known, nor can we be sure of thinking clearly and coming to accurate conclusions in every case, but we can work toward those goals. Reading books that make you think is one very good way to help yourself grow mentally. Journaling is another way: by letting ourselves write down our thoughts freely, without suppressing or editing anything, we learn more about how we think and can identify ways in which we can improve our thinking.

Most of the time, if we have trouble thinking clearly about something, the trouble is rooted in our feelings. Most of the time, in turn, problems with our feelings are rooted in our habitual thoughts and beliefs! If we believe we are inadequate, for example, that belief becomes the anchor for feelings of depression and misery, and these in turn help feed the belief that we are inadequate. Breaking this vicious circle requires the clarity of sight that Readers seek to develop. Journaling, affirmations, and meditation—three of the essential skills you began practicing when you first started on the path of the Golden Section—are all helpful in learning to create and use this inner clarity.

We all function as Readers in our lives. We constantly read our surroundings, the people we encounter, and our own thoughts and feelings and experiences. Sometimes it is appropriate for us to read aloud from those sources of wisdom, for the benefit of others. At other times it is appropriate for us to remain silent. It is said we speak with other people with our mouths, but we speak to animals by our actions and with plants with our emotions. It is further said we speak with the Divine through our thoughts and we listen with our inner ear. Our inner ear is our intuition.

Your work as a Doorkeeper

While you prepare yourself to become a Reader, you remain a Doorkeeper as well as a Cleric. Continue to make prayer a part of your daily life, and to perform the sacraments of blessing and naming whenever you have the opportunity to do so.

You may also find it useful to look for opportunities to open doors for other people and to discover what doors other people are opening for you. Make it a regular practice to examine the troublesome people in your life. They trouble you because you have a door to open for them or because they have a door to open for you. Meditate and ask the Divine to reveal to you what door you need to open for each troublesome person or what you need to do so they will open the door for you. Pray for Divine guidance in dealing with them. Try to determine what it is you need to do for all the troublesome people in your life.

Another approach is to ask these people what you can do to serve them, or to help them; ask them what they need from you. It often happens that when we ask other people how we may help them, the Divine intervenes in their lives to help us identify what we need to do to resolve the current situation.

Opening a door is always providing a service. Sometimes all we need to do is point these individuals in the right direction because the door is already open. Other times we need to do something, provide some service for them. Often times all we need to do is learn how to accept them and forgive them so they can get on with their lives.

Whatever is required to open the door for them is our responsibility to discover. It's part of the work we need to do to resolve this situation, to balance the karma. There's no judgment involved. You're not a bad person because you have a debt to repay. The troublesome people in your life are not bad people just because you owe them something, because you need to open the door for them.

The sacrament of teaching

Many Christian churches practice the sacrament of Confirmation for people who have been baptized, whether as infants or as adults. In Confirmation the individual commits to membership in the church and to obedience to its teachings. The Universal Gnostic Church does not do this as its teachings consider that commitment to be a wholly personal matter between the individual and the Divine.

For those individuals who wish to make a public commitment to their faith, clergy of the Universal Gnostic Church are encouraged to use the sacrament of naming, which was discussed in the previous lesson and is one of the duties of the Order of Doorkeeper. The ceremony of naming, when used for this purpose, can be expanded by giving the person receiving the sacrament a space to state, to the clergyperson and to anyone else present, the commitments that he or she is making at that time.

The sacrament assigned to the order of Reader, rather, is the sacrament of teaching. Once you have completed the requirements for this minor order and become a Reader, you have the right and duty to perform the sacrament of teaching for other people under the auspices of the Universal Gnostic Church.

The sacrament of teaching may be performed in many ways and there is no set ritual for it. By this stage in your studies you have learned many things that you can teach to others, and it is your place to pass on those teachings to anyone who wants to receive them. Please note, however, that you cannot require anyone to learn from you. No matter how much you think that someone needs to learn what you have to teach, you must give them the freedom to choose otherwise.

In many situations the best way to teach is simply to teach by example. If you live a life of wisdom in harmony with the Divine, those who need what you have to teach and are ready to receive it will be drawn to you. There is an old proverb that says, "When the student is ready, the teacher appears." It is just as true that when the teacher is ready, the student appears. If no students appear for you, consider the possibility that you are not yet ready to teach them. If this upsets you, you may want to teach people as a way to exercise authority over them and to bolster your own ego. This does no good for you or anyone else.

Ceremony of commitment for a Reader

Once you have put at least a month into the work outlined above you will have completed the traditional requirements to become a Reader in the Universal Gnostic Church. This title confers no special privilege upon you. It doesn't give you the right to tell other people what to do, or to preen yourself on your supposedly superior spiritual status. It simply reflects a commitment on your part to enter into a relationship with the Divine and to bless the world around you.

The ceremony is a way of honoring your acceptance of the work before you. It's a ceremony of commitment, which affirms that you understand what it means to be a Reader and accept whatever the Divine may ask you to do. In order to perform this ritual, you will need all the same items you used in the earlier ceremonies of commitment.

The ritual consists of seven steps.

First, open a lodge of the Golden Section Fellowship in the usual form. Make sure the holy water, holy oil, and written prayers and vow (if you are using these) are close to the altar of your lodge.

Second, say a prayer in which you thank the Divine, using whatever name you prefer, for all the gifts bestowed upon you. Ask for Divine blessings upon the lodge and yourself. Ask the Divine to be present and to accept you as a Reader. You may use a spontaneous prayer, or write out a prayer in advance.

Third, vow to the Divine to uphold the Office of Reader and to serve as a Reader to the best of your ability; and then ask the Divine to assist you in keeping and fulfilling these vows. This also may be spontaneous, or written out in advance.

Fourth, purify yourself with holy water. This is done by dipping your fingertips into the water and using them to moisten your eyelids, your ears, your nostrils, and your lips with holy water. Dip your fingers into the water between each of these. While purifying yourself, say something like this: "I purify my senses so that I will be able to perceive the spiritual realms of existence, so help me (name of the Divine being used)."

Fifth, anoint yourself with holy oil on the eyelids and on the lips. In anointing yourself, say something like: "I anoint myself to perform all the duties of a Reader, so help me (name of the Divine being used)."

Sixth, say a prayer of thanksgiving, thanking the Divine for the blessings that have been conferred on you. Then take your seat and meditate for a time on the experience of the ceremony.

Seventh, close your lodge in the usual way.

Please note that the point of this ritual is not to impress anybody, including yourself. You gain no special status nor any authority over other people by becoming a Reader. The point of the ceremony is to humbly and sincerely communicate with the Divine, take your vow, and bless the work the Divine will hereafter ask of you. Having completed the ceremony you are a Reader. You are now ready to go forth and do such work as the Divine asks of you.

Completing the fourth circle

Plan on devoting at least one month to learning and practicing the work of this circle. Before you go on to the next circle, review all the material assigned to the fourth circle and be sure you understand it and have practiced it correctly. Remember that you can always take more time to complete the work if you wish. When you are ready, proceed to the fifth circle.

CHAPTER FIVE

The fifth circle

The work of the fifth circle follows the same pattern and rests on the same foundations as that of the circles you have already mastered. The basic practices you learned in *The Way of the Golden Section*, the three exercises given in the previous section of this book, the visualization of the temple before you begin your meditation and the visualization of your guardian angel afterwards: these remain the core practices for your development. Once again, the temple visualization changes, and you will add another vortex into the second step of the energy-awakening exercise, after the temple visualization and just before you massage the back of your head. The fourth step in working with the palm centers for blessing and healing, the fourth of the Gnostic Lessons, and the fourth of the minor orders, the order of Healer, also belong to this circle. We'll proceed through these one at a time.

Visualizing the temple: Phase five

The workers have again been busy with your temple: the roof and ceiling are in place, and the windows and doors have been installed. The three windows on each side may be of any design you choose, whether clear or stained glass, while the circular window on the end you are facing is clear, and has the outer emblem of the Order worked into the glass, as shown in the diagram. The door is a plain door of wood.

Temple design 3

The temple is now complete in its external form. It still needs an altar and certain other furnishings, and it also waits for the invocation of the spiritual forces that will flow through it.

During the time you spend on this circle, spend five minutes or so visualizing the scene described above. As you did with the earlier temple visualizations, see and sense this scene as clearly as possible, and then release the imagery and proceed to the awakening of the first five of the seven vortices, as described below.

The fifth vortex

The fifth of the vortices we will be working with is located at the base of the throat, above and behind the notch in your collarbone. As the first two vortices relate to the material plane, the third to the etheric plane, and the fourth to the astral plane, this vortex relates to the mental plane, the plane of meanings, intentions, and values. Human beings currently have astral, etheric, and material bodies, but we are still evolving our mental bodies. Many people find, therefore, that this vortex requires more work than the ones you have activated already.

The throat vortex relates to communication and also to the mental properties of understanding and reflection. It has a special relationship with the genital vortex; these two energy centers are like the two poles of a magnet, and from them the fields of subtle energy that surround you spread out like a magnetic field. Once both are activated, you will find that your ability to perceive things intuitively becomes more developed.

In this fourth stage of the work, you will start by visualizing the two knee vortices spinning, giving them three breaths each; then proceed to visualize the genital vortex spinning, again for three breaths; and then go on to the liver vortex, and visualize that spinning while you take three breaths. Then visualize a star at the location of your throat vortex. Begin spinning that in a clockwise direction, the same direction as the other vortices. Breathe in and out while visualizing the spinning star, until you have taken seven slow, steady breaths. Then release the imagery and go on to the rest of the energy-awakening exercise.

Blessing with the palm centers

The work you have done so far with the palm centers has completed the preparation for healing and blessing work using these centers. At this point, if you wish, you may continue daily practice with the exercises you have been given already—the awakening of the palm centers and the circulation of the solar and telluric currents through the body—or you may scale back these practices to as little as one session a week, which need not be done at the same time as your other practices. The choice is yours.

One application of the training you have received that is especially relevant to the work of this circle is the art of blessing using the life force radiating from your palm centers. Before you begin learning how to do this, review the material about the sacrament of blessing in the chapter that deals with the second circle. The form of blessing discussed there is basic, and forms a foundation to any more advanced blessing practice.

Blessing is an intention. It is the purest form of positive intention, the effort to bring down the grace and joy of the highest planes of being and make them manifest in some part of the realm of ordinary human experience. That intention can be given shape in many ways, on the material plane or on any other plane. The use of the palm centers for blessing is one of these.

The easiest way to learn this is to bless holy water or holy oil using the palm centers. To do this, when next you are about to prepare holy water or holy oil, put the material you are about to bless (salt in the case of holy water, the oil itself in the case of holy oil) in a glass, pottery, or stoneware container—*not* metal, which will disperse the subtle energies you will be using. Pray to the Divine in whatever way you prefer. If you wish, you may also visualize your guardian angel or guardian genius and ask for its help.

Once you feel ready to proceed, awaken your palm centers and fill yourself with the solar and telluric currents in the way you learned in the previous circle. Then place your hands on either side of the salt or oil, with the palms inward. Visualize the energies of the solar and telluric current flowing from your palm centers into the salt or oil, the solar current from the right hand, and the telluric from the left. Imagine them fusing to create the lunar current in the salt or oil, so that it glows brilliant white, with greater and greater intensity, until it is too bright to look at directly.

Hold that image in your mind for a time, and while you do so, repeat the words of blessing you have chosen, saying them clearly and distinctly and concentrating on each word as you say it. When you have finished with the words of the blessing, take your hands away from the salt or oil and seal the palm centers in the usual way. Then, if you are blessing holy water, add the salt to the water and repeat any appropriate words of blessing as you do so.

This same approach can be used to bless anything else, including people. Be sure to ask for and receive consent before giving someone a blessing empowered by the palm centers, as such a blessing tends to be unexpectedly forceful!

Using oil blessed using this method is especially recommended for the sacrament of anointing, discussed later in this circle.

The order of Healer

The fourth of the minor orders was in ancient times given the title of Exorcist, and in some churches it still retains that title. Many centuries ago, however, the difficult and spiritually challenging practice of exorcism was transferred to the priesthood, and to specially trained and qualified members of the priesthood at that. For this reason, in the Universal Gnostic Church, this order has been renamed Healer.

The spiritual and religious dimension of healing has been seriously neglected in modern times, not least because the medical industry is jealous of its prerogatives (and of course its income) and has therefore tried to drive every alternative mode of healing out of existence. This is a source of great suffering in our time, because—though there are certainly forms of illness and injury that take place mostly or entirely on the material plane—there are many more that extend higher up the ladder of being.

Illnesses that are rooted in blocked life energies, tangled emotions, mistaken beliefs, or unfulfilled spiritual hungers cannot be cured by medicines or surgery. At most, physical methods of healing can provide temporary relief from the material consequences of such illnesses. As a Healer, it is your duty and privilege to use the traditional methods of prayer, blessing, and anointing to help yourself and others. Once you are prepared to do so by the circles ahead, you may also use energy healing with your palm centers to help heal yourself and others.

There are many other modes of spiritual and energetic healing. Your ceremony of commitment as a Healer will not qualify you to practice any of them. However, if you have learned another method of healing before now, or go on to become qualified in some other healing method hereafter, you may practice that as part of your ministry as a Healer. Always remember that your practice must be conducted in accordance with the laws of the country and locality where you live. Doing anything else reflects badly on the Universal Gnostic Church and the Golden Section Fellowship, and can also land you in a great deal of legal trouble. Check your local laws before you begin to practice spiritual healing for anyone else's benefit!

Please also review the instructions given in previous Gnostic Lessons on the sacrament of blessing, and continue to practice it daily. Remember the more you bless, the more you will be blessed. Remember also that many people who approach healers for help need nothing more esoteric than someone who will listen to their concerns and give them a blessing.

You have already learned that you are more than your material body, that you are more than your emotions, and that you are more than your ideas and thoughts. Now you must learn that you are more than your spiritual gifts and capacities. There is a spark of the Divine at the center of your being, around which all the other aspects of yourself have formed. Make an effort to become aware of that spark of the Divine. Turn your attention to it, especially but not only when you pray. The more attention you direct toward it, the more it will reveal itself to you, and in the process you will become more and more aware of what you really are, a child of the Divine.

Hearing and intuition

The order of Healer is associated with the faculty of hearing. When you listen with your outer ear, you hear the words and the emotions behind those words. But when you listen with your inner ear you also hear the awareness, intentions and beliefs of the speaker. True, you are already hearing those things with your subconscious mind, but you become a much more powerful Healer if you tune into your inner self and listen also with your inner ear.

Practice listening more and more with your inner ear by listening to the Divine. In your meditation practices, make it a habit to include your devotions and then listen for the response of the Divine. Listen and you will hear. As you practice listening to the Divine you'll gain many new insights into yourself and the people, places and things in your life. You can even open communication with other spiritual beings. You decide which of these you wish to invite into your life.

The more you open your inner ear, the more opportunities you'll have to serve others and the more you'll hear of what they have to say. Practice hearing what others and the Divine wish to communicate to you until you've mastered the art of hearing more deeply than before.

Hearing and listening are called the lost arts. Busy people seldom take the time to really listen, to really hear another person. Since most everybody is busy, very few people are left to listen and to hear. One important part of being a Healer is to listen, because healing requires a mastery of the art of listening to others. We cannot hear as long as we're talking. We can listen only by being silent and tuning into the other person with our mind, heart and soul. Then we hear. We truly hear.

Make it a daily practice to stop and listen to other people. Hear what they're saying with their words, feelings, awareness, intentions, and beliefs. Listen and when you're ready to speak, wait and listen some more.

Continue to listen until you understand the communication on every level, then formulate your thoughts and finally speak.

This is a big order, but if you really want to serve others, remember you serve them best by listening. You epitomize the best of being a Healer by listening intently and with focus.

Practice hearing what other people are really saying. Remove the filters of your own awareness, intentions and belief systems to the best of your ability. Open yourself to true communication by listening to others.

If we take the time to listen to other people, we will also hear. We'll hear far more than we expected and in much greater detail than we may have needed. But hidden within this load of garbage are pearls of wisdom. We just need to listen. Sometimes the Divine will communicate to us in this way, while at other times the Divine will communicate to us in the silence between the words we hear. We just have to listen.

We can use this same technique to speak with our guardian angel or guardian genius, or with other spiritual beings. The only difference between speaking with the Divine and speaking with other spiritual beings is our intention. If you intend to commune with the Divine, you will. If you intend to communicate with our guardian angel or guardian genius, you will. If you intend to communicate with other spiritual beings, you will. Formulate your intention clearly and remember that it is your ability to hear clearly, rather than their ability to speak, that puts limits on the communications you can receive.

Communicating with beings other than the Divine and our guardian angel or guardian genius involves certain risks. Not every incarnate human being can be counted on to tell you the truth or to act honestly and fairly, and the same thing is true of disembodied beings. What modern Druid teacher Philip Carr-Gomm has called the three mystic senses of the Druid—common sense, a sense of proportion, and a sense of humor—should always be cultivated by anyone who interacts with spiritual beings. Regular practice of the Sphere of Protection is also helpful here, as it charges your aura in a way that repels the more dubious kinds of spirits and attracts beneficial entities.

Decide what communications you want with the "other side," set your intentions and meditate. Ask for Divine guidance and protection as you practice and you will receive it. Meditate and listen. Listen for those you are trying to contact and you will hear. With a little practice, you will hear.

Your work as a Reader

As you study to become a Healer, it is important to remember that you remain a Cleric, a Doorkeeper, and a Reader. Continue to make the practice of daily prayer part of your life, alongside the daily practices of the Golden Section Fellowship, and perform the sacraments of blessing, naming, and teaching as often as you are called on to do so.

Now is a good time to go back and review all the practices you are doing. Read the instructions over again and make sure you haven't forgotten any of the details. If you started working with a set of practices, and let them lapse after a while, consider taking them up again. You do yourself a very great service if you do these practices every day even if it means putting your advancement on hold while you make up for lost ground. You do yourself a great disservice by neglecting the foundations of your practice in a mistaken rush toward advancement.

As a Reader you are well advised to pay attention to your senses of smell and taste on both the mundane physical level and with your intuitive mind. Continue to develop these senses as you continue to advance on your spiritual path. You're also well advised to continue moving toward health on all the planes by keeping up the practices you have already been taught. Take the time to review these materials if you need to do so. The work that is before you depends upon these things.

The sacrament of anointing

Oil is traditionally used in anointing though there is no prohibition against using other liquids such as water, salt water, vinegar, wine or any other solution. It is possible to do anointing with a paste rather than a liquid, but this is rarely done. When using a paste, some material is usually pulverized into a powder and oil is added to make the paste. The sacrament is called anointing whether an oil or a paste is used.

Anointing can be done in a manner similar to baptism or naming a child. It is usually done as part of another ceremony but may be done alone as a blessing. Prayers are usually offered before and following the anointing. The first prayers are to prepare the candidate for the anointing and the latter for thanksgiving.

Anointing may be done to a person, animal, plant, mineral, or any object of any kind. The material being anointed and the material used for anointing is not critical to the ceremony. The intention of the person doing the anointing is. When it comes to anointing, intention is almost everything. It is wise to plan your anointing ceremonies accordingly.

Anointing can be used for spiritual healing. So can prayer, laying on of hands, palm center healing, and anything else the Divine inspires you to use. The only admonition that applies is to do nothing against the will of the individual or the Divine. Keep in mind that the Divine will never ask you to do anything harmful; the Divine will always ask you to do everything according to the Law of Love.

Healing prayer is unction and unction is healing prayer. Extreme unction or supreme unction is healing prayer for the dead or dying.

Healing prayer is best done with the heart rather than the head according to most mystics. The more emotion we put into our prayers the more impact they have on the dead and the dying. Our emotion is not to convince the Divine of anything, for the Divine hears us no matter what. Our emotion is for the dead and the dying so they know they are loved as they pass over into the other world. This makes their transition very much easier.

Ceremony of commitment for a Healer

Once you have put at least a month into the work outlined above you will have completed the traditional requirements to become a Healer in the Universal Gnostic Church. This title confers no special privilege upon you. It doesn't give you the right to tell other people what to do, or to preen yourself on your supposedly superior spiritual status. It simply reflects a commitment on your part to enter into a relationship with the Divine and to bless the world around you.

The ceremony is a way of honoring your acceptance of the work before you. It's a ceremony of commitment, which affirms that you understand what it means to be a Healer and accept whatever the Divine may ask you to do. In order to perform this ritual, you will need all the same items you used in your earlier ceremonies of commitment.

The ritual consists of seven steps.

First, open a lodge of the Golden Section Fellowship in the usual form. Make sure the holy water, holy oil, and written prayers and vow (if you are using these) are close to the altar of your lodge.

Second, say a prayer in which you thank the Divine, using whatever name you prefer, for all the gifts bestowed upon you. Ask for Divine blessings upon the lodge and yourself. Ask the Divine to be present and to accept you as a Healer. You may use a spontaneous prayer, or write out a prayer in advance.

Third, vow to the Divine to uphold the office of Healer and to serve as a Healer to the best of your ability; and then ask the Divine to assist you in keeping and fulfilling these vows. This also may be spontaneous, or written out in advance.

Fourth, purify yourself with holy water. This is done by dipping your fingertips into the water and using them to moisten your eyelids, your ears, your nostrils, and your lips with holy water. Dip your fingers into the water between each of these. While purifying yourself, say something like this: "I purify my senses so that I will be able to perceive the spiritual realms of existence, so help me (name of the Divine being used)."

Fifth, anoint yourself with holy oil on the ears and the palms of your hands. In anointing yourself, say something like: "I anoint myself to perform all the duties of a Healer, so help me (name of the Divine being used)."

Sixth, say a prayer of thanksgiving, thanking the Divine for the blessings that have been conferred on you. Then take your seat and meditate for a time on the experience of the ceremony.

Seventh, close your lodge in the usual way.

Please note that the point of this ritual is not to impress anybody, including yourself. You gain no special status nor any authority over other people by becoming a Healer. The point of the ceremony is to humbly and sincerely communicate with the Divine, take your vow, and bless the work the Divine will hereafter ask of you. Having completed the ceremony you are a Healer. You are now ready to go forth and do such work as the Divine asks of you.

Completing the fifth circle

Plan on devoting at least one month to learning and practicing the work of this circle. Before you go on to the next circle, review all the material assigned to the fifth circle and be sure you understand it and have practiced it correctly. Remember that you can always take more time to complete the work if you wish. When you are ready, proceed to the sixth circle.

CHAPTER SIX

The sixth circle

The work of the sixth circle builds further on what will by now be a familiar foundation. The basic practices you learned in *The Way of the Golden Section*, the three exercises given in the previous section of this book, the visualization of the temple before you begin your meditation and the visualization of your guardian angel afterwards are as important here as in the previous circles. Once again, the temple visualization changes, and you will add a sixth vortex into the second step of the energy-awakening exercise, after the temple visualization and just before you massage the back of your head. The first set of instructions in healing with your palm centers, the fifth of the Gnostic Lessons, and the fifth and last of the minor orders, the order of Acolyte, also belong to this circle. We'll proceed through these one at a time.

Visualizing the temple: Phase six

The temple is now complete! As you sit in your chair, looking toward the round window, you see an altar before you, and on it the altar gear of a lodge of the Golden Section Fellowship: the altar cloth, the three bowls containing salt, water, and either incense or dried herbs, the compass and straightedge, and the four elemental working tools: the book, the cup, the wand, and the pentacle. Beyond the altar, to either side of the window, are two pillars, a black one to the left and a white one to the right, as shown in the diagram.

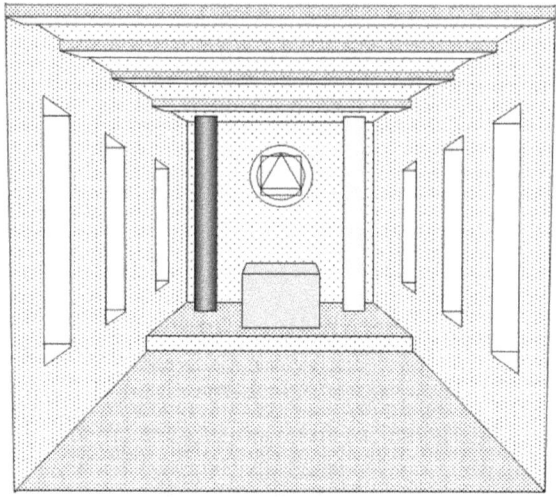

Temple design 4

These need not be the only decorations in your temple. You may include any sacred symbols or images that are meaningful to you. For example, if you are Christian, you should certainly consider including a cross or a crucifix in the temple; if you are Hindu or Pagan, a statue of a god or goddess may be included, and so on. This is your personal sacred space. Decorate and equip it so that it will be right for you.

During the time you spend on this circle, spend five minutes or so visualizing the scene described above. As you did with the earlier temple visualizations, see and sense this scene as clearly as possible, and then release the imagery and proceed to the awakening of the first six of the seven vortices, as described below.

The sixth vortex

The sixth vortex we will be working with is located at the pineal gland. This is one of the two centers you have been working with since you initiated yourself into the Golden Section Fellowship. The pineal gland, as you have already learned, is called the Eye of Revelation in some occult traditions. When it is activated, it enables the individual to tap directly into the spiritual plane and to receive guidance and insight from far above the human level. It therefore plays a central role in the quest for wisdom, revelation, and enlightenment central to the work of the Fellowship. You have been awakening it slowly and gently since your initiation. The work of this circle will take that further and speed up the process of inner awakening.

In this sixth stage of the work, you will start by visualizing the two knee vortices spinning, giving them three breaths each, and then proceed to visualize the genital vortex spinning, again for three breaths. Proceed to the liver vortex, and then to the throat vortex, giving each of these three breaths and imagine them spinning clockwise. Then visualize a star at the location of your pineal gland, roughly halfway between the tops of your ears. Begin spinning that in a clockwise direction, the same direction as the other vortices. Breathe in and out while visualizing the spinning star, until you have taken seven slow, steady breaths. Then release the imagery and go on to the rest of the energy-awakening exercise.

Self-healing with the palm centers

To use the palm centers for healing, it is best to start by learning how to heal yourself. Like all forms of energy healing, the method you are about to learn works best when practiced regularly when you are in normal health, as its great strength is as a preventive to help keep you from becoming ill. If you are already ill, you may need to make use of material-plane methods as well as energy healing, and if your illness is at all serious, you should certainly seek help from a licensed health care provider in addition to using energy healing on yourself. Energy healing is not a replacement for material-plane healing modalities. It works best when used to resolve imbalances before they reach the level of serious illness, to work with minor illnesses of a kind that most people ordinarily treat with home remedies, and to benefit chronic conditions of the sort that rarely respond well to treatment on the material plane. For these uses, regular treatments of energy healing can be extremely valuable.

The practice of healing with the palm centers involves a sequence of passes made by the hands. These passes have two distinctive features. First, your hands never touch your material body (or the body of the person you are treating), remaining always a few inches away from the material body. Second, each pass is followed by a quick shaking of the hands, as though you were scattering drops of water from your fingertips. The first of these allows the healing energies to flow freely from your palm centers to the etheric body of the patient, whether this is you or someone else. The second clears away excess energy and sheds unbalanced energies you might otherwise pick up in the course of treatment.

Before you do any form of healing work, whether for yourself or for others, awaken the palm centers using the method you have been taught, tracing the elemental symbols on each palm and then joining the palms, and go on to circulate the solar current downward and the telluric current upwards three times. These preliminary steps awaken the healing energy in your palm centers and prepare you for the healing work.

Passes for self-healing

The basic sequence of passes for self-healing is as follows:

First, place the hands side by side above the top of your head, perhaps an inch from your scalp, with the fingers pointing backward. The hands should be relaxed, not tense. Draw the hands slowly down and forward in front of your face, leaving the hands parallel and side by side, and maintaining roughly the same distance between the palms and your face, and continue down the front of your neck. When your hands reach the top of your chest, allow them to rotate so that the fingertips point toward each other; in this position, draw them down the front of your body to the level of your hips, and then down the thighs to the knees. Here the fingertips turn down, and you pass the hands down the front of your lower legs, as low as you can comfortably reach. End the first pass by sweeping the hands forward a foot or so, and then giving them a good crisp shake to clear them of excess energy. Repeat this pass a total of three times.

Second, return the hands to the top of the head, with the fingertips close together but the palms angling diagonally outward, toward your temples. Draw them slowly down and forward along the sides of your face, in front of the ears, and then down your neck to the shoulders. At this point they rotate as before, so that the fingertips point to one another, but some inches should lie between them—the exact distance will depend on the breadth of your chest. Pass them down your chest to your hips and then down your thighs, passing over areas just outside the areas you covered in the first pass. By the time you reach your knees, your fingertips will naturally have rotated forward; here you allow them to turn downward and pass down the outside front of each lower leg as far as you can reach. Finish the same way as you did the first pass, and repeat this pass a total of three times.

Third, return your hands to the top of your head, but now the fingertips are pointing toward one another above the crown of your head and your palms are to the side, above your ears. Draw your hands slowly down the sides of your head and neck, then rotate them around the front of your shoulders so that they end up at the sides of your chest, as close to your armpits as the conformation of your arms and body will permit, with the fingers pointing down. Move them down your sides to your hips, down the outside of your thighs, and down the sides of your lower legs as far down as you can reach. Finish the same way as you did the first two passes, and repeat this pass a total of three times.

Fourth, return your hands to the top of your head, and put them in the same position as they were at the start of the third set of passes. This time, though, move the hands slowly backward, down the back of your head and neck, turn them so that the fingers are pointing downward, and sweep them outward along the back of your shoulders, ending with a quick shake. Put them behind your back, palms facing your back and fingertips pointing toward each other, and slide them as far down your back as you can without hitting the seat of your chair; sweep them out along your hips and end the movement again with a quick shake. Finally put them under your thighs, fingertips pointing toward each other, and slide them down the backs of your legs, letting the fingers turn downward naturally as you go; reach down as far as you can, and then end by sweeping the hands outward and shaking them again. Repeat this whole sequence a total of three times.

Fifth, place your left arm comfortably on your left thigh, palm up. Put your right hand above the top of your head, palm down and then draw it slowly down the left side of the head and neck, over the left shoulder, and down the inside of the left arm, right out past the fingertips. Shake the hand briskly, then repeat the movement a total of three times. Then turn the left arm over, so that your hand rests on your thigh with the palm down, and repeat the same movement with the right hand three times. Then switch hands, doing three passes on the inside of the right arm and three passes on the outside, using the left hand.

Sixth, give your hands a thorough shake, and then place your hands in front of your forehead with the palms facing your forehead and the fingertips pointing toward each other. Let your hands curve a little, so that the fingertips bend inwards toward your forehead without touching the skin. Take three slow breaths, allowing the energy to flow from your fingertips into the pineal center in the middle of your head. Then move your hands down to solar plexus level, keeping them in the same position, and take three more slow breaths, allowing energy to flow into the solar plexus. When you have finished, draw your hands away and shake them briskly three times.

Seventh, bring your hands together in front of your belly, with the fingers pointing down and the backs of the hands facing each other. Raise them up the midline of your body as you breathe in, allowing the hands to change position naturally until the fingers are pointing up. Rotate the hands so that your palms are facing outwards, spread your fingers slightly, and sweep them out and down. Let them come to rest at your sides; pause until you feel the energy flowing out of them, and then give them a good shake. Repeat this whole process three times. This concludes the basic sequence of passes for self-healing.

Working with specific illnesses

The seven passes provide a good general balancing for your entire body, and will help maintain it in good health. If any part of your body feels unwell, however, you may wish to direct more focused energy toward it. This is done between the fifth and sixth passes.

Exactly what you will do should depend on the quality of the illness or imbalance you sense in your body. Some conditions are a product of not enough life force, while others are the product of too much life force congested in some part of the body. These have different symptoms and are treated differently.

Conditions that involve too little life force feel cold and empty, physically and energetically. The cold, hollow feeling many people get in their sinuses or chests immediately prior to coming down with a cold is a good example of this feeling. To treat a condition of this kind, place one or both hands an inch or so away from the part of the body where the cold and empty feeling is apparent, and concentrate on having the solar and telluric energies flow into that part of the body, filling it with light and life. Do this for as many breaths as you wish, depending on how serious the lack of energy feels, and then continue with the rest of the healing process.

Conditions that involve too much life force feel hot, congested, and inflamed, physically and energetically. The heat and swelling around an injured joint are good examples of this. To treat a condition of this kind, use one or both hands to stroke over the part of the body where the hot inflamed feeling is present. The stroking should always follow the same natural pattern of flow used in the seven passes, that is, away from the top of the head and toward one of the extremities. For example, a condition on an arm that involves excessive nwyfre should be treated by strokes in the air just above the skin that start just above the ill or injured place and pass over it, moving down toward the hand. Repeat this as many times as you wish, depending on how serious the congestion feels, and then continue with the rest of the healing process.

Practice the self-healing passes at least once each week during the time you spend in this circle. You may do this work more often—as often as once a day, if you wish.

The order of Acolyte

The training of the Acolyte, the fifth and last of the minor orders, is dedicated to the sense of touch and the soul. Our soul is our true self. It is our soul that lives and experiences life through our physical, mental, emotional, psychological and spiritual bodies. Here's a little story that explains how the soul works:

Jack and Jill were called into the office one day. They were told that because of cutbacks they were being laid off. But if they wanted to wear an animal costume, they would not only stay on the payroll, they would receive an increase in salary and a big bonus in one year.

They looked over the options. Jack decided to wear the bear costume and Jill decided to wear the eagle costume. Both costumes fit just fine. The only problem was that they were literally sewn into their costumes and had to wear them 24/7. They could attend to their daily chores, eat and drink, but they were unable to leave their costumes for the duration. Hence the large bonus they both looked forward to receiving.

Neither Jack nor Jill was able to shave but they could brush their teeth and continue to kiss each other among other things. All in all, it turned out to be a pretty good arrangement for them except for one little problem. The problem was that after a couple of months Jack considered himself to be a bear and Jill thought she was an eagle. Their minds had shifted from being a human in a costume to being the costume.

So it is with our soul. Our soul decides to incarnate in a physical body, and so it does. The next thing you know, our soul begins to believe it is our body. It forgets it is a soul in a body and it begins to believe it is the body.

Here's the great secret: We are our soul. Our soul is us. We have always been our soul and we still are. In our ignorance we came to believe we are our ego, our personas and our body. But we are still our soul. We're just wearing a costume with many faces.

We are, all of us, a soul walking around in a three-layered costume. The outermost layer is our physical body, brain and our many personas. The next layer is our ego and the emotions and mind that comes with it. Our inner layer is our soul itself. But it turns out this is just a costume worn by our eternal spirit.

One way to understand the work of awakening is to see it as a process of three marriages. The first marriage is when we integrate all our fragmentary personas (partial personalities) into a unity and wed the resulting personality to our ego. The second is when we raise up our ego and marry it to our soul. To raise up our ego really means that we become our soul and recognize we are our ego and we are our soul and they are one and the same thing operating on different levels. Then we bring our ego up to the level of the soul and the marriage is accomplished. Finally, the third alchemical marriage occurs when we are able to become our spirit and raise up our soul to marry our spirit. Once you have accomplished this you will become fully integrated as the spirit the Divine created, but you will become more than you were before you created a series of costumes called your soul, ego, personas, and body.

This can also be understood by way of elemental symbolism. Earth unites with Water to form a Higher Earth and this evolves into Higher Water. Higher Water unites with Fire and evolves into Higher Fire. Higher Fire unites with Air and evolves into Higher Air. Higher Air unites with Spirit and becomes Enlightened Spirit. Meditate on these sentences; they can reveal much to you.

The two explanations just given describe the same process. They both mean that we can become aware of the possibilities of spiritual development, set our intentions, and using our faith in ourselves and the Divine, move ever upward toward the light of true knowledge. This is our spiritual path and we give it many names and describe it in many different ways.

As Acolytes we are to ponder these things.

Your work as a Healer

By now I hope you do not need to be reminded that you are still a Cleric, a Doorkeeper, a Reader, and a Healer as you approach your ceremony of commitment as an Acolyte. Daily prayer should be a regular part of your schedule of practices, and the sacraments of blessing, naming, teaching, and anointing should be familiar to you from repeated practice. The palm center healing you have just been taught can also be an important spiritual practice. You can accomplish a great deal of good in the world by continuing to do these things.

As you continue to pray, to perform the sacraments, and to do the healing work you have learned, consider expanding your understanding of healing. Illness in the narrow sense of the word is not the only thing that a Healer can heal through prayer, blessing, and anointment. Any time the world as we experience it falls short of the infinite understanding and bliss that is the nature of the Divine, healing may be called for. Along with sick bodies, many of us have sick hearts, sick minds, and sick souls. Those, too, can be healed by calling on the Divine using the sacramental means you have already learned.

Always remember, however, that consent is essential in healing. Many people do not want to be healed. Sometimes this is appropriate, as when a person realizes on some level that an illness is important as a way of working through difficult karma. Sometimes it has motives that are less positive. Nonetheless you have neither the right nor the power to heal someone who does not want to be healed. Always ask, always make sure the healing you offer is welcome.

You will also encounter people who say they want to be healed but will do everything in their power to cling to their illness. Here your work is more straightforward. Bless them, anoint them, and pray for them to receive as much healing as they are willing to accept. Silent prayer is usually helpful in such cases!

Each of us can only carry the burden of healing the world so far. Be careful not to exhaust or overload yourself in trying to help others. Healing yourself is also an appropriate use of your healing abilities. Praying for yourself is as important as praying for others. Treat yourself and others with equal kindness and you will help make the world a kinder place. Bless yourself and others equally and you will help make the world a more blessed place.

Life as sacrament

You have learned and practiced the sacraments of blessing, naming, teaching, and anointing, the four formal sacraments that are assigned to the minor orders of the Universal Gnostic Church. Three other sacraments are reserved for priests, priestesses, and bishops. The sacraments of marriage and of divine service are reserved to the priesthood, and the sacrament of holy orders—the rites that pass on the priesthood of the Universal Gnostic Church—is reserved to bishops.

The custom of reserving the sacrament of marriage to the priesthood is purely legal in its origin, since most jurisdictions require ordination as a priest or priestess in order to officiate at a wedding. In reality, of course, the sacrament of marriage is performed and consecrated by the two people who say "I do," and the officiant merely ratifies what has already happened in the hearts of those to be married. But the legal forms must be followed.

The custom of reserving the sacrament of divine service to the priesthood has deeper roots. Divine service is our term for the ceremonies and actions by which one person helps others make contact with the Divine. Those ceremonies and actions can take place in a church building on Sunday mornings, though they can equally well happen in other places and at other times. It is one thing to work toward closeness with the Divine oneself, and a much more complex, challenging, and important thing to help make this happen for others. The full training of the Gnostic priesthood is necessary in order to do this effectively, compassionately, and with a clear sense of the possibilities and problems that it entails.

The custom of reserving the ordination of priests to bishops, finally, is a simple reflection of the fact that a priest or priestess must have a complete working knowledge of the traditions of the Universal Gnostic Church in order to fulfill the priestly function. A bishop is an experienced and learned priest or priestess who has mastered the entire body of Universal Gnostic tradition in theory and practice, and so can supervise the instruction and ordination of priests and priestesses.

The three sacraments just named, therefore, are not among the functions of Acolytes or anyone else holding one or more of the minor orders. Despite what was said above, however, recipients of the minor orders are not limited to the four sacraments of blessing, naming, teaching, and anointing. These are the four formal sacraments assigned to those orders, but the formal sacraments are only one small part of the world of sacramental action.

What is a sacrament? Any action, performed with intention, that reconnects the world of ordinary experience with its roots in the Divine.

Any action can be a sacrament. Every action can be a sacrament. As you pursue your studies in preparation for your ceremony of commitment as an Acolyte, see how many activities in your daily life you can perform with intention in order to reconnect your world to the Divine. All of life can become a sacrament. You may not feel ready to make this a goal of yours yet, but be aware of the possibility, and be ready to make your actions function as a sacrament any time you realize that a conscious awareness of the presence of the Divine is needed.

It is by the correct use of our heart and intellect we are able to continue along our own spiritual path. By seeing things as they really are, we are able to honestly evaluate what next needs to be done. As we come to see, hear, taste, smell and touch the Divine in all things, as we come to intellectually understand all of creation, we are able to commune more and more with the Divine.

Touch and intuition

If you've been working with the practices you've already learned in these lessons, very likely you're already noticing things you never tasted, smelled, felt, heard or seen before. Your third eye or pituitary center is beginning to open and you're becoming more aware of life. If you haven't noticed these things, continue your practices and you soon will.

Acolytes are assigned the sense of touch. Acolytes are encouraged to become more aware of the texture, temperature and moistness of the objects they touch. Texture can be smooth or rough and everything in-between. Temperature can be hot or cold, and anything in-between. Moistness can be wet or extra dry and everything in-between.

During the month or more you spend on the Acolyte training, pay attention to the people and things you touch. Pay attention to the feel of the person or thing. Allow your tactile sense to improve and become more sensitive to the things you touch. As you pay attention to your tactile sense, your sense of touch, you'll notice that your senses of taste and smell also continue to improve. As your senses of sight, hearing, touch, taste and smell continue to improve in the physical world, your psychic senses will open and improve as well.

Your psychic sense of touch, or clairtangence, can be improved by using it daily. Relax your mind and body, enter into rhythmic breathing for a few minutes, and then pick up an object and hold it in your hands. Tune into the object and see what ideas come to your mind. Write them down in your practice journal, include the date, and then do your best to forget about the session for a couple of weeks. Pick up the same object several weeks later and see what comes to your mind. Then review your previous notes and add to them.

You'll find that for some objects you remember the previous session very well. For these objects you'll pick up additional information. With other objects, you will find that you don't remember the previous session, and in this case you'll also pick up additional information. Look for ways to make these pieces of information come together as smoothly as if you did remember the first session. Always review the notes you've made in your practice journal, however, because sometimes you will find yourself "remembering" things you didn't perceive in the earlier session. In cases like these, intrusive thoughts or feelings are often involved. When your clairtangence is working well, the object will give you additional information about the truth it gave you the first time. Sessions like these do more to validate your psychic sense of touch than anything else.

We encourage you to continue working to develop your psychic senses as you work through the Acolyte training. Work on your senses of sight, hearing, taste, smell and touch. Continue working daily on improving your physical senses of sight, hearing, taste, smell and touch. As these senses become more sensitive, your psychic senses will also improve. As a corollary, the more you work on improving your psychic senses, the more your physical senses will also improve.

As you work with objects, in addition to ideas that come from the object, you'll also pick up feelings from other people. Become aware of these feelings and make a record of them in your practice journal. After a few times, not more than a half-dozen times, it's time for you to work at picking up impressions from other people. Choose objects you know people have handled. Record the feelings you obtain. When it's appropriate to do so, you may even confirm these feelings with the person who left them on the object.

This process is called psychometry and it's the basic psychic sense used when working with other people. All you need is an object the person normally keeps near them, like a set of car keys. But any object with the person's vibration imbued in it will work just fine. Breathe deeply, relax, become centered and pick up the object. Tune into the object and relate the feelings you pick up. Write it down for future reference.

The same process can be used when you know you're going to shake the hand of a person. Breathe deeply and relax. Become centered then approach the person and shake his or her hand. Tune into the vibrations of this individual. Later when you get a few minutes you can tune in more deeply and pick up what you need to know.

Practice the lessons assigned to this circle and the order of Acolyte. Expand your knowledge of these things through your private studies and devotions.

The Acolyte is commissioned to continue following the spiritual path he or she has started and to start evaluating ritual. The Acolyte should take it upon him or herself to study various kinds of ritual for various purposes and integrate what he or she finds of value into his or her own ritual practices. The office of Acolyte is an office of the student, and more particularly the student of ritual. All ritual is intended to be a direct link with the One Source for a particular reason. The Acolyte is counseled to discover the reason behind every ritual, to uncover the purpose of the ritual. This is done as a step preparatory to writing one's own rituals for specific purposes. You may not feel that you are ready to write ritual, but the preliminary steps are being undertaken at this stage, and you may find it useful to begin sketching out ideas for rituals of your own creation.

Ceremony of commitment for an Acolyte

Once you have put at least a month into the work outlined above you will have completed the traditional requirements to become an Acolyte in the Universal Gnostic Church. This title confers no special privilege upon you. It doesn't give you the right to tell other people what to do, or to preen yourself on your supposedly superior spiritual status. It simply reflects a commitment on your part to enter into a relationship with the Divine and to bless the world around you.

The ceremony is a way of honoring your acceptance of the work before you. It's a ceremony of commitment, which affirms that you understand what it means to be an Acolyte and accept whatever the Divine may ask you to do. In order to perform this ritual, you will need all the same items you used in your previous ceremonies of commitment.

The ritual consists of seven steps.

First, open a lodge of the Golden Section Fellowship in the usual form. Make sure the holy water, holy oil, and written prayers and vow (if you are using these) are close to the altar of your lodge.

Second, say a prayer in which you thank the Divine, using whatever name you prefer, for all the gifts bestowed upon you. Ask for Divine blessings upon the lodge and yourself. Ask the Divine to be present and to accept you as an Acolyte. You may use a spontaneous prayer, or write out a prayer in advance.

Third, vow to the Divine to uphold the office of Acolyte and to serve as an Acolyte to the best of your ability; and then ask the Divine to assist you in keeping and fulfilling these vows. This also may be spontaneous, or written out in advance.

Fourth, purify yourself with holy water. This is done by dipping your fingertips into the water and using them to moisten your eyelids, your ears, your nostrils, and your lips with holy water. Dip your fingers into the water between each of these. While purifying yourself, say something like this: "I purify my senses so that I will be able to perceive the spiritual realms of existence, so help me (name of the Divine being used)."

Fifth, anoint yourself with holy oil on the crown of your head and the base of your throat. In anointing yourself, say something like: "I anoint myself to perform all the duties of an Acolyte, so help me (name of the Divine being used)."

Sixth, say a prayer of thanksgiving, thanking the Divine for the blessings that have been conferred on you. Then take your seat and meditate for a time on the experience of the ceremony.

Seventh, close your lodge in the usual way.

Please note that the point of this ritual is not to impress anybody, including yourself. You gain no special status nor any authority over other people by becoming an Acolyte. The point of the ceremony is to humbly and sincerely communicate with the Divine, take your vow, and bless the work the Divine will hereafter ask of you. Having completed the ceremony you are an Acolyte. You are now ready to go forth and do such work as the Divine asks of you.

Completing the sixth circle

Plan on devoting at least one month to learning and practicing the work of this circle. Before you go on to the next circle, review all the material assigned to the sixth circle and be sure you understand it and have practiced it correctly. Remember that you can always take more time to complete the work if you wish. When you are ready, proceed to the seventh and final circle.

CHAPTER SEVEN

The seventh circle

The work of the seventh circle finishes the process of building on the foundation laid down in the earlier books in this sequence and developed in the previous circles of this book. The basic practices you learned in *The Way of the Golden Section*, the three exercises given in the previous section of this book, the visualization of the temple before you begin your meditation and the visualization of your guardian angel afterwards remain central to this stage as to those you have already experienced. The lessons on developing your intuition are already complete and the temple visualization has already taken on its final form. You will learn how to heal others using the palm healing method in this circle, and you will add the seventh and final vortex into the second step of the energy-awakening exercise, after the temple visualization and just before you massage the back of your head. If you feel you are ready, you may also add a further stage to the work with the seven vortices—a circulation of life force that connects your throat and genital vortices with other centers along the front and back of your body.

Since there are only five minor orders in the Universal Gnostic Church tradition, the Gnostic Lesson assigned to this stage of the process was very brief, encouraging Acolytes to review the work of the previous lessons and consider whether or not they wish to go further, and begin studies for the priesthood or priestesshood. Since the Golden Section Fellowship teaches occultism rather than religion, it does not train priests and priestesses, though you may take up training of this sort on your own if you wish to do so.[12] You should certainly consider reviewing all the work you have done so far, in the six previous circles and also in the first two books of Golden Section occult instruction. All this previous work and all the teachings associated with it will be central to the work to come.

The core practice for this circle, however, is a ceremony of a kind that was once practiced in occult lodges and religious churches and temples alike: a ceremony of communion. This also comes from the Universal Gnostic Church tradition, and in that tradition it was not restricted to the priesthood or priestesshood; any person who wished to perform it was (and still is) free to do so. It differs in important ways from the communion ceremony most people think of these days, the one practiced by sacramental Christian churches. Those differences will be explained fully as we proceed. First, though, the other new practices for this circle should be introduced.

Visualizing the temple: Phase seven

The temple visualization has the same form in this circle that it had in the sixth circle. The chief difference is that now you are free to leave your chair, in your imagination, and move around the temple. You will be doing this during the ceremony of communion mentioned above, so it will be helpful to get some practice doing it beforehand.

Except when doing specific kinds of spiritual work, as specified later in this circle, you should remain in the naos or nave when you move around the temple. Entering the adytum or sanctuary brings you into direct contact with the spiritual energies that have begun to flow through your secret temple. You will be doing this when you perform the communion ceremony described shortly, and in certain other contexts to be explained later. Outside of those contexts, remain in the nave.

---

[12] It is not required, or even recommended, that you should do this in the Universal Gnostic Church or in any of its offshoots. There are many schools these days offering priestly training in the independent sacramental movement and other alternative traditions, and you may pursue any of these that appeals to you.

If you wish, you can change the order of your practices at this stage of the work and enter the temple in your imagination before you perform your Sphere of Protection. Most people find that it works best to sit in the chair facing the altar, visualize the temple, and then stand up and begin the ritual, imagining all the while that you are doing it in the temple. You can also do the lodge opening and closing ritual in the temple and your own lodge space at the same time. This has certain subtle effects which will be explained later in this section.

During the time you spend on this circle, spend five minutes or so visualizing the temple as described earlier either before you perform the Sphere of Protection or before you begin awakening the seven vortices. As you did with the earlier temple visualizations, see and sense this scene as clearly as possible, and then release the imagery and proceed either to the Sphere of Protection or to the awakening of the seven vortices, as described below. (If you do the temple visualization before you start your Sphere of Protection, you don't need to repeat it afterwards; just sit down once the Sphere of Protection is completed, take three slow breaths to relax and center yourself, and begin the awakening of the seven vortices.)

The seventh vortex

The seventh and final vortex we will be working with is located in the front of the head, between and behind the eyebrows. It is linked with the pituitary gland; though the material structure of that gland is a little further back in the head, its etheric and astral structures extend forward to form the "third eye" that plays so important a role in the esoteric traditions of Asia.

This vortex, like the pineal vortex, is linked with planes far above those where humanity is currently active. Where the pineal vortex relates to the spiritual plane, the third eye vortex connects to the causal plane, the plane immediately below the Divine. Immensities of spiritual evolution lie between each of us and the point at which we will begin to perceive the causal plane even indirectly. This stage of the exercise is thus starting the process of setting out another set of foundations on which we will build in the far future.

While we are still incarnate human beings, however, this vortex has another function. By awakening it, we speed up the development of the five psychic senses discussed in an earlier circle: clairvoyance, clairaudience, clairflairance, clairgustance, and clairtangence. All of these function through centers in the etheric and astral body located in the front of the head, above and behind the eyes. Daily work with the seventh vortex will activate these centers and improve your ability to perceive things on the planes above matter.

In this seventh stage of the work, for now, you will start by visualizing the two knee vortices spinning, giving them three breaths each, and then proceed to the genital vortex, the liver vortex, the throat vortex, and the pineal vortex one after another, visualizing them spinning clockwise, giving them three breaths each. Then visualize a star at the location of your third eye vortex. Begin spinning that in a clockwise direction, the same direction as the other vortices. Breathe in and out while visualizing the spinning star, until you have taken seven slow, steady breaths. Then release the imagery and go on to the rest of the energy-awakening exercise.

The circulation of light

One further stage of the work with the vortices can be added at this time, or at any other time you feel ready to do so. This is a circulation of life force through the body. It is also done as part of the preparation for your daily meditation, but it is done after all the other preparatory stages—after you have visualized the secret temple, awakened the seven vortices, massaged the back of your head, filled your body with light while tensing the muscles, and then relaxed the muscles. It is at this stage, just before any prayer you may offer and before the meditation proper, that you circulate the life force through your body.

Various ways of circulating life force through the subtle channels of the body have been practiced in different occult and spiritual traditions around the world. This version, which comes from the same Rosicrucian traditions that introduced the seven vortices and the rest of the energy-awakening exercise, has three features that set it apart from most other examples of the same sort. The first is that the circulation follows a figure-8 pattern through the head and body, crossing at the throat center. The second is that the circulations do not use the channel at the center of the spinal cord. Instead, it uses one or the other of the two nerve channels that flank the spinal column on either side.

The central spinal channel is the most powerful of the channels for subtle energy in the material body. but also the most risky to awaken artificially, and Western occult teachings consistently (and sensibly) avoid working with it directly. Instead, work with other channels clears the nervous system and the corresponding structures of the etheric body clears away blockages so that the awakening of the spinal channel can happen in a healthy, balanced, and spontaneous manner. The figure-8 pattern and the directly of flow through the side channels both further that clearing process.

The last difference between the method taught here and most other ways of circulating life force is that there are two versions, one for occultists and one for mystics. What does this latter distinction mean? Simply that some people are more comfortable relating to the spiritual realms of existence using their minds, while others are more comfortable doing this with their emotions. Neither of these is better than the other; neither is right and neither is wrong; the simple fact is that people vary, and that variation is reflected in certain aspects of spiritual practice.

Circulation—occultist

88 THE WAY OF THE SECRET TEMPLE

If you are an occultist by nature, you tend to approach the spiritual realm with your mind, trying to make sense of your experiences in spiritual practice by thinking about them. In this case, the circulation you should practice begins at the base of the spine and goes up a channel to the left of the spinal column—not through the spinal column itself. It rises up in this way to the base of the neck, and then goes forward to the throat center. From there it rises straight up through the midline of the neck and head, passing between the pineal and the pituitary gland, to the crown of the head, and from there down the back of the skull to the base of the skull. Then it proceeds to the throat center again, and then goes straight down the midline of the body to the genital center, and then down and back to the base of the spine, completing the circulation.

Circulation—mystic

If you are a mystic by nature, you tend to approach the spiritual realm with your heart, trying to make sense of your experiences in spiritual practice by attending to your feelings about them. In this case, the circulation you should practice is nearly the exact opposite of the occultists' circulation. From the base of the spine, it goes forward and up to the genital center, and then rises straight up the midline of the body to the heart. From there it goes forward to the front of the chest and up from there to the throat center, and then to the base of the skull, and up and over the skull to the crown of the head. Then it descends straight down, passing between the pineal and pituitary glands, to the throat center again. From there it goes back to a channel on the right side of the spine—not the spinal column itself—and descends through that channel all the way to the base of the spine, completing the circulation.

The differences matter, because the occultist and the mystic work with different energy centers in the etheric and astral bodies. The occultist circulation is intended to direct subtle energies primarily to the centers in the head, while the mystic circulation is intended to direct the same energies primarily to the heart center. Again, neither of these is better than the other; it is purely a matter of which one best suits your personal orientation toward spirit. The one strict rule is that you must choose one and stay with it; mixing the two can cause problems with your adrenal glands and damage your health.

Whichever circulation you choose, practice it daily at the end of the preparatory exercise, right after you have relaxed your tensed muscles. Take it slow and easy; start each circulation on an inbreath, but at first, take as many breaths as you need to complete each cycle. For the first six months, do only three complete circulations in your daily practice, counting each circulation as beginning and ending at the base of your spine. After six months, you can increase this to seven circulations, but no more. As your subtle bodies get used to the circulation, energy will start flowing spontaneously and gently through the pattern you've traced out, and this will complete the process of clearing blockages away from your energy body. Let this happen at its own pace, relying on the seven circulations in each day's meditation practice to guide and direct it. Step by step, over the months and years ahead, this practice will lead you to wisdom, revelation, and enlightenment.

Healing others with the palm centers

By the time you begin work on this circle you have practiced the method of self-healing given in the last circle several times. In the process, you have begun to learn through direct experience how this form of healing works, what it can do, and what increases or decreases the healing effect of this method of working. Even if you have not noticed these things consciously, your subjective mind has done so, and will have adjusted your technique to benefit your material, etheric, and astral bodies.

This has another beneficial effect. Most people have blockages and imbalances in their subtle bodies that interfere with their ability to do energy healing. Through the work you have already done with self-healing, and also your work with the vortices and your practice of the energy-awakening exercise and the circulation of light these have been lessened or even eliminated. The traditional saying "Physician, heal thyself" is worth remembering here; too many people who need healing themselves focus too much on healing others without taking care of their own problems first. This tends to make them more vulnerable to illness, and it also means that they tend to pass on their own illnesses and imbalances to others, leaving their patients worse off than before.

Thus it is important that you continue practicing the self-healing passes you learned in the previous circle, as well as the other practices you have learned. As a rule, you should do self-healing more often than healing for others. This may sound restrictive or selfish, but it is based on a great deal of practical experience. When you do a palm center healing for another person, it is your responsibility to see that your energies are as clean and balanced as possible, since those energies will be in contact with theirs. You also need to be sure you clear away any imbalances you pick up from the people you treat, so that the imbalances cause no harm to others that you may treat, or to you.

Legal issues in healing

If you practice spiritual healing for another person, you will be stepping into a minefield made much more difficult than it has to be by the influence of the medical and pharmaceutical industries on modern society. Laws in many countries prohibit anyone but licensed professionals trained in the officially approved medicine of our day from helping other people in any way related to health. In the United States today, even if no money changes hands, describing what you are doing as "healing" or "curing," or referring to someone you are helping as a "patient," can risk legal charges and the possibility of a prison term. Unreasonable as this is, it is the current reality, and you will need to live with it until such time as the legal and social environment changes. Whenever you practice this work with other people, therefore, you should refer to it as "spiritual energy work," and under no circumstances should you claim to be able to heal, treat, or cure any physical ailment or injury, or even suggest that you will try to do so.

Absurd as these restrictions may seem, they have an ethical dimension that is not wholly unreasonable. As a novice practitioner of spiritual energy work, you have only a very little experience with a subtle and profound art, and your ability to help others will be sharply limited by your lack of experience with the techniques. This work needs to ripen gradually, and that takes time and practice. Until your skills have risen to the necessary level, it is unethical as well as legally risky to claim to be able to heal, treat, or cure illnesses or injuries.

For these same reasons, you should never accept money or anything else of value in return for performing this work. For the time being, as you study and practice these teachings, the benefit you get in exchange for your efforts is experience with the spiritual healing process, which is more than enough to make it worth your while. Even after you have mastered this method of healing, keep in mind that in many jurisdictions the laws against accepting money for unapproved methods of healing are strict, and can land you in more legal trouble than you want to deal with. It is much simpler to treat the abilities that you will develop as a gift that you can share freely with others, as part of your work as an initiate.

A further ethical issue is that you should never do healing work for someone who does not consent to it. In most cases this is not an issue, since you will normally only do spiritual energy work for people who have agreed to participate. In the case of a child, an unconscious person, or anyone else not able to give legally valid consent, for legal as well as ethical reasons you need to ask for, and get, the consent of the person's legal guardian before proceeding.

Finally, you should never physically touch a person you are helping during a session. In today's society, touching another person carries with it a great many tangled personal, ethical, and legal issues that are best left alone. For similar reasons, a man who performs this work for a woman who is not a relative by birth or marriage, or any person performing this work on a child other than his own, should have another person present at all times during the session.[13]

---

[13] These suggestions may seem old-fashioned to modern ears, but given the current state of gender relations, they are still wise to follow.

The method of working

When you are ready to perform spiritual energy work for someone else, the first thing you need to do is explain to the person you are helping what you will be doing, and what they can expect to experience. Explain that you will not be touching them physically at any point, but that you will be directing energy from the cosmos to balance and harmonize the body of subtle energy that surrounds and enlivens the material body. Let them know that they may perceive tingling, a sense of warmth, or other mild sensations, and encourage them to let you know if anything becomes uncomfortable in any way during the session. Should you be asked to perform a session for a person who is unconscious or for a young child, or for anyone else who cannot give consent, explain these things to the person who has arranged for you to do the work.

If at all possible, the person to be treated should sit on a plain armless chair, such as a dining room chair or a folding chair, with feet flat on the ground and hands resting on thighs. The chair should be placed so that you can stand in front of it, behind it, and to the right side. Encourage the person you will be treating to sit a little forward, so that their lower back does not touch the back of the chair, and ask them to close their eyes, breathe normally, and relax. If the person is not able to sit in a chair for whatever reason, adjust the passes accordingly.

Once they are ready, tell the person that you will need a minute or so to prepare yourself, and that you will tell them when you begin the session. Sit in another chair facing the person, awaken your palm centers, and draw in the solar and telluric currents in the way you have already learned. When you are ready, let them know that you are about to begin.

At this point, place your hands comfortably in front of you, palms facing the other person, and allow the solar and telluric currents to flow from your palm centers toward them. You will feel the energies meeting resistance at first, as though you were pushing against something heavy and unyielding. Continue to draw telluric energy up from below you and solar energy down from above you, and let them flow out through your hands. After a few seconds, you will begin to feel the energy begin to flow as you make contact with the other person's etheric and astral bodies. Maintain the flow for a time, until you feel no more resistance.

Next, rise from your chair and approach the other person. Tell them that you are about to make passes with your hands over their body, and remind them that you will not touch them physically. Standing before the person, make passes with both hands down the front of the body from head to waist level, keeping your hands 6 to 12 inches away from the body. Do this three times with the hands side by side in front of the body, then move your hands out to the sides and make three more passes; continue moving your hands apart and performing three passes until the whole front and sides of the body, from head to waist, have been covered by your passes. As before, give the hands a quick shake after every pass.

Now kneel down and do the same thing from the waist to the feet, starting with the hands side by side in front of the other person and making three passes, then proceed outward from there until his hips, legs and feet have been covered by your passes. Continue to shake the hands to clear them of energy after every pass.

Stand up again. Explain that you will be standing behind them; go around behind the chair, and do another series of passes. This time, however, you start with passes down the sides of the head, shoulders and arms, down to hip level. Do this three times, then move your hands a little further back and repeat with another three passes. Do this until you perform three passes with your hands side by side on either side of the other person's spinal cord. Again, shake the hands after each pass.

Now move to the other person's right side, and explain that you are about to charge the energy centers of the subtle body. Start by placing your right hand in front of the person's forehead and your left hand behind the back of the head, again leaving 6 to 12 inches between your hands and the body. Holding your hands steady, concentrate again on the flow of the solar and telluric currents through your body and hands, and allow the energies to flow into and through the pineal center until there is no sense of blockage or imbalance. Move your hands down to the level of the solar plexus, your right hand in front of the chest and your left behind the middle back, and repeat the process with the solar plexus. Remember to shake your hands after charging each of the centers.

Stand up again and explain that the working is almost over, and you simply need to clear away excess energy from his energy body. This is done with a series of broad sweeping motions down from above the head, well away from the body, with a crisp shake of the hands after each motion. When you are finished, let the other person know, and explain that you need to close off the energy flows in yourself to conclude the working. Encourage them to relax as you do so. Sit in your chair, and close in the way you have already learned.

Healing at a distance

This same process may be done when you are unable to go to the person who needs healing. Healing at a distance may be performed in one of two ways, depending on your level of skill. The simplest version of the spiritual energy working for another person at a distance is done by activating the palm centers while facing toward the other person, no matter how far away the distance between you. Once the palm centers are activated, just as in the first part of the ordinary method, place your hands comfortably in front of you, palms facing the other person, and allow the solar and telluric currents to flow from your palm centers toward the other person. Concentrate on the idea that the energies of the solar and telluric currents are flowing across the distance to come into contact with the other person's subtle bodies, charge it with energy, and restore it to balance and wholeness. Maintain the energy flow for as long as you desire, or sense to be necessary.

The more complex and difficult form of the spiritual energy working for another person at a distance is done by placing a chair as though the other person was with you, visualizing the other person sitting in the chair, and maintaining that visualization as strongly and clearly as possible while performing the full working just as though the other person was present. Since the life force is present everywhere and in all things, no barrier separates you from anyone else in the world, and the work you do will have a definite effect even across vast distances. This is among the reasons why it is essential to attend to the ethical dimension of this work, and to perform it only when the recipient of the work has given his permission.

A form of initiation

It is also possible to use these same methods to pass on a form of initiation to other members of the Golden Section Fellowship. Like most forms of initiation, this one is a way to speed up the changes that regular spiritual practice causes in the material and subtle bodies of the student. It is therefore not necessary to receive this initiation from another person in order to confer it. The work you have already done as a student of the teachings has prepared you to pass on some of what you have achieved to others.

This initiation can be given to anyone who has studied the teachings, taken up the practices, and performed the self-initiation ritual in

The Way of the Golden Section. It is important not to confer it on anyone who has not proceeded at least this far in the work of the Fellowship. The energies set in motion by the initiation interact with the changes already set in motion by the practices covered in the first stage of the Fellowship's training, and may cause awkward mental and emotional states in someone who has not yet done that training.

To perform the initiation, you will need two chairs and a private room. Start by having the candidate (the person who is to be initiated) sit in one of the chairs and enter meditation. Sit down in the other chair and formulate your secret temple around you. Next, clear the space and awaken your own subtle bodies by performing the initiate's version of the Sphere of Protection, imagining yourself doing this inside the temple all the while. Do this so as to include the candidate in the cleared space and in the temple. Afterwards, sit back down in the chair and awaken your own palm centers in the way you have been taught.

Then rise and stand on the right side of the candidate. Place your right hand in front of the candidate's solar plexus, 6 inches or so in front of his or her body, and your left hand an equivalent distance behind his or her back at a point directly behind the solar plexus. Once you have done this, send the two currents streaming inwards from your hands into the candidate's solar plexus center. See and feel the currents forming a sphere of white light, intense and luminous as a star. Do this for several minutes at least with the intention of charging the solar plexus. Continue this as long as it feels appropriate to do so.

Then raise your hands until your right hand is in front of the candidate's forehead and your left hand behind the back of the candidate's skull, again about 6 inches away. Repeat the same process, visualizing a sphere of brilliant white light in the center of his head. Again, do this for several minutes, concentrating on charging the center, and continue as long as it feels appropriate.

Once you have finished, step back, turn both your palms to face the candidate, and bless him or her silently or aloud. When you are ready, release the imagery of the secret temple and congratulate the new initiate. This completes the process of the initiation.

This initiation is very helpful in the early intermediate stages of the Golden Section work, when the candidate has learned the core practices and performed the self-initiation ceremony but still has much of the work of the Fellowship still to do. It gives the candidate considerable assistance in attuning to the One Life and learning to concentrate and direct his or her thinking processes, and it helps awaken the solar plexus center and pineal center, the two most important energy centers used in the Fellowship's work.

A note on practice

You may or may not have the opportunity to do healings or initiations for anyone else during the time you spend working in this circle. As already explained, you should continue to perform the self-healing exercise given in the previous circle at least once each week. If you have the opportunity to practice spiritual energy work or perform initiation for other people during the time you spend in this grade, by all means do so, and pay attention to the differences that are made by having another person's energy involved in the work. If not, simply keep practicing the self-healing passes. The universe will provide you with opportunities to use your healing and initiatory abilities when the time is right.

Introduction to the communion ceremony

The communion ceremony is the central practice of the third, innermost level of the Golden Section Fellowship, which is communicated in this book. Like equivalent ceremonies in other spiritual traditions, it centers on a ritual process by which food and drink become the vessels for spiritual forces, and are then consumed by the participant in the ceremony. In the process, it draws on core aspects of the ancient temple rituals discussed elsewhere in this book.

To avoid confusion, it may be helpful to stress at the beginning that this ceremony is not a Christian Communion ritual, nor is it modeled on the Communion rites of any of the Christian churches. Ceremonies in which bread and wine are used as receptacles for spiritual forces go back far into antiquity, and have been used by many traditions unrelated to Christianity. The Golden Section communion ceremony is derived from these more ancient models—specifically, from a set of ceremonies practiced in the ancient mysteries and echoed in fragmentary form in the legends of the Holy Grail.[14]

That point needs to be made and remembered, because now and again people tend to confuse the Golden Section communion ceremony

---

[14] I have discussed some of this lore in my recent book *The Ceremony of the Grail*.

with the Mass, Communion, or Lord's Table ritual practiced in Christian churches. If you happen to be Christian, you can certainly practice the ceremony that follows and invoke Christ while doing so, but it is in no way a substitute for, or even a partial equivalent of, the Christian rituals just named. It is a different rite with a different purpose. The similarities between this communion ceremony and the Christian rituals are like those between a backpacker's poncho and the chasuble worn by a Catholic priest at Mass. Granted, they are similar in form, but their purposes are noticeably different!

What, then, is the purpose of the Golden Section communion ceremony? Put simply, it is a ritual method of invoking the two great currents of spiritual energy that move through the world of our experience—the solar current and the telluric current—and bringing them together to create the lunar current, the source of wisdom, revelation, and enlightenment. It can be done for other people but it is normally a solitary ritual, part of the personal spiritual work of initiates of the third degree of the Golden Section Fellowship, and it forms a central part of the work of inner development that awaits you as you proceed beyond the three degrees.

The communion ceremony has another dimension, however. Its effects are not limited to the person who performs it, or for that matter to the people who are present when it is performed. They spread out from the lodge where the ceremony is performed to affect the surrounding area and ultimately the whole world. Each time the ceremony is performed, the solar and telluric currents flow together and send a pulse of the lunar current radiating out in all directions. This is equally true of other, similar rituals, including Christian communion rituals, and explains part of the positive effect these have when they are performed properly.

How often should you plan on performing this ceremony? That depends on you. In *The Way of the Four Elements* you learned rituals to celebrate the solstices and equinoxes, and the communion ceremony can be combined with these. Instructions for the combined ceremonies are given in full in the Appendix below. (The communion ritual replaces the simpler sharing of food and drink you learned at that stage of your training.) These four rituals are a good minimum for your repetitions of the communion ceremony. On the other hand, you can perform it more often than this if you wish, as much more often as you decide and your circumstances permit.

Requirements of the ceremony

As noted above, the communion ceremony is not an act of public worship. You are free to invite others to witness the work and partake of the communion, but you are also free to celebrate it in solitude, and for most people this is the most practical option. Those whose attendance is necessary for the ceremony, those with whom the initiate communes, are not human beings but the holy powers of Nature: in particular the solar and telluric currents, the powers of the elements, and whatever deities you may choose to invoke.

The material requirements of the ceremony are relatively simple. It should be performed in your Golden Section lodge room, and the chair, the altar, and the usual altar furnishings are needed in the ceremony. In addition, however, you will need a chalice and a paten (a small plate for the bread) to occupy the center of the altar. These should be of pottery or stoneware if possible, to represent the Earth, and may be of whatever design or color appeals to you personally. Chalices and patens of the kind used in Catholic or Orthodox Christian practice are emphatically not suited to this ceremony, and the elaborate arrangements made to keep the bread and wine of the Christian service separate from the rest of the material world are equally out of place.[15] The bread and wine used in the Golden Section ceremony, after all, are not the body and blood of a deity—they are simply bread and wine into which certain spiritual influences have been infused. In addition to the chalice and paten, two cruets or small vessels, for wine and water, respectively, are used. These should also be of glass, pottery, or stoneware if possible.

The material substances that are to be consecrated and consumed in the ceremony are bread and wine—bread as a vessel for the telluric current, and wine as a vessel for the solar current. The wine is mixed with water, to represent the alchemical fusion of the red and white dragon currents, symbolized also by the Red and White Wells of Glastonbury that play a significant role in the legends of the Holy Grail. It is best for the bread to be made from some kind of grain, and the wine fermented from some kind of fruit. Wheat and grape are by no means required in

---

[15] Many Christian chalices and patens are either made of gold or plated with gold, so that the bread and wine of the ceremony only comes into contact with gold. This is not appropriate for the Golden Section ritual, which works with energies that are present in all of material existence.

this ritual, though they may certainly be used if desired. If you have dietary issues that make either grain or wine inadvisable, however, you may use whatever substitutes will work best.

It is customary in the Universal Gnostic tradition to receive communion by intinction—that is, by having each person who partakes of communion take a portion of bread in his or her hand, dip the bread into the wine in the chalice, and then place the wine-soaked bread in his or her own mouth. This is considerably more sanitary than sharing a common cup, and considerably less cumbersome than using a separate cup for each participant.

Furthermore, intinction has an important symbolic meaning. Anyone who partakes of the communion by intinction is an active participant, not merely a passive recipient in the ceremony. He or she personally performs the crucial action of the ritual, the union of the material vessels of the solar and telluric currents.

In addition to the items just named, a book should be chosen to provide a brief reading for meditation. The lection, as the reading is called, can be whatever you prefer. It should be relatively short, no more than a page or two at most, and generally less than that. Its purpose is to provide seed thoughts for meditation. Any book you find relevant to your own spiritual practice can be used for this purpose.

Before the opening of the ceremony, the lection text is set next to your chair. The chalice is placed near the altar and the paten placed atop the chalice. The bread is set on the paten, and the cruets of wine and water are placed close to the chalice. You can then proceed to light the incense and begin the lodge opening ceremony.

The communion ceremony

First, imagine yourself within your secret temple and then perform the lodge opening ceremony, seeing yourself inside the temple all the while. When you go to the altar in the opening ceremony, see yourself as entering the sanctuary or adytum of the temple.

Second, return to the naos or nave, and sit in your chair facing the altar. Open the Lection text, and say: "The lection for this ceremony is from (*name of book or other source*)." Then read the text aloud. It should be read slowly, to allow you and anyone else present to pay close attention to each word and phrase, and gather one or more seed thoughts for meditation. When it is done, pause and then say: "May the holy powers enlighten my mind (*or:* our minds)."

Third, set the text aside, and enter into meditation. At least five minutes should be spent in meditation, and you may continue it as long as you find appropriate.

Fourth, when the meditation is finished, rise, enter the adytum or sanctuary, and approach the altar. Say: "Let this lodge be prepared for a ceremony of communion." Now move the straightedge and compass over to the right side of the altar, and reverse the compass so that its points are away from you. Place the chalice with the paten at the center of the altar, and put the two cruets near it, as shown in the diagram below.

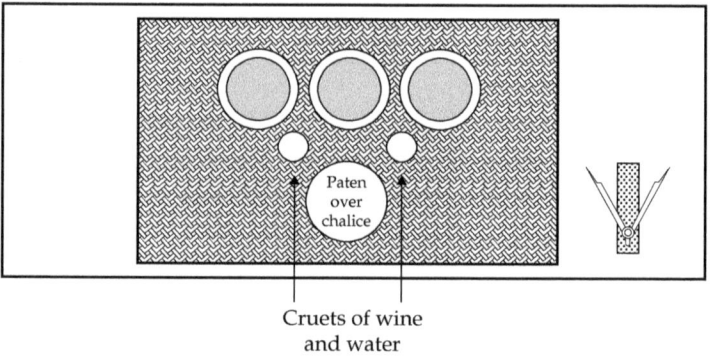

Altar diagram 2

Fifth, say the following words:

> I now invoke the mystery of communion, that common unity that unites all beings throughout the worlds. All beings spring from One; by One are they sustained, and in One do they find their rest. One the hidden glory rising through the realms of Abred; One the manifest glory rejoicing in the realms of Gwynfydd; One the unsearchable glory beyond all created being in Ceugant; and these three are resumed in One.[16]

---

[16] The terms Abred, Gwynfydd, and Ceugant are taken from the Druid tradition. Abred (pronounced Ah-bred) is the realm of material incarnation. Gwynfydd (Gwin-vith) is the realm of spiritual existence entered by those who have learned the lessons of material incarnation. Ceugant (Kye-gant) is the realm of the Divine.

Sixth, extend your hands over the altar in blessing. Say:

> From that One, through the radiant Sun and the nurturing Earth, through the powers of the elements made manifest in wind and light and rain and soil, the harvest and the vintage come forth for the sustenance of all. May the powers of the elements and the spirit of life now likewise hallow this bread and this wine, that they may be fitting vessels for the light of heaven and the life of Earth.

Seventh, lower your hands. A prayer may be inserted here, calling on any deity or deities that you wish to preside over the working. Whether or not this is done, the next step is to say:

> Holy powers of living nature, may your blessing abide in this work, and radiate from it to bless the living Earth and all that lives upon her; to bless all who hold Nature in reverence; to bless the Golden Section Fellowship and all its members; and to bless all who participate here today.

If you wish to direct the blessings of the work toward a particular person, place, or purpose, go on to say the following: "May your blessing extend especially to (name)," and if appropriate, describe the situation that you feel needs the blessing of the powers. Whether or not this is done, proceed to say: "In the presence of the One, with the help of the powers, let the mystery of communion be made manifest in space and time, in this place, in this time."

Eighth, lift the paten from atop the chalice with your left hand, and with your right, move the chalice to the right. Place the paten with bread in the center of the altar. Take the bread in both hands, raise it silently in offering, and then replace it on the paten. Say: "I invoke Spirit Below." If you wish, you may say instead: "In the name of (deity), I invoke Spirit Below," calling upon whatever deity you wish to invoke in relation to the telluric current. In either case, proceed to say the following:

> Power of the deeps, holy mystery in the Earth's heart, receive this offering! As the grain rises from the buried seed of winter to flower and fulfill the circle of its being, so let a ray of the telluric current arise and fill this bread with the power and blessing and grace of the Earth.

Pause at this point, and visualize a ray of green light rising from the heart of the Earth, through the altar and paten, into the bread. Make this visualization as clear and intense as possible. Then say: "The telluric current has arisen."

Ninth, take the cruets, and pour water and wine into the chalice. Take the chalice in both hands and raise it in offering high above the center of the altar. Say: "I invoke Spirit Above." If you wish, you may say instead: "In the name of (deity), I invoke Spirit Above," calling upon whatever deity you wish to invoke in relation to the solar current. In either case, proceed to say the following:

> Power of the heights, holy mystery in the Sun's heart, receive this offering! As the radiance of summer shines upon the grape to ripen and renew the circle of its being, so let a ray of the solar current descend and fill this wine with the power and blessing and grace of the Sun.

Pause at this point, and visualize a ray of golden light descending from the heart of the Sun into the cup and the wine. Make this visualization as clear and intense as possible. Then say: "The solar current has descended."

Tenth, lower the chalice and hold it in your right hand. Take the bread from the paten with your left hand, and raise it above the chalice. Say: "From above to below, from below to above, the two currents are awakened." As you recite the words below, dip the bread into the wine. Visualize a sphere of brilliant white light, like a full Moon, taking shape around the chalice as the bread and wine come into contact. Say:

> In their union, the union of Sun and Earth, let the lunar current be born, the wondrous child and jewel of light. Let its radiance extend to all beings, that the land may be blessed to fruitfulness, that the ancient wisdom may be made known to the worthy, and that all who seek wisdom, revelation, and enlightenment shall find them.

Eleventh, take the bread from the wine and partake of it. If anyone else is present and wishes to partake of the communion, place a piece of bread in their hands and then hold the chalice so that they may dip the bread in it, and partake. When all who wish to partake of the communion have done so, drink any wine that remains, place the chalice on the empty paten, leave the adytum or sanctuary, and return to the chair.

Twelfth, sit for a few minutes, or longer if you prefer, contemplating the ceremony and sensing its effects. Then rise, move the chalice, paten, and cruets off the altar, replace the straightedge and compass in the center of the altar in their usual positions, and proceed with the lodge closing ritual. When you have finished the ritual, allow the image of the secret temple to fade out of your mind.

The temple as mesocosm

The ceremony just described is ordinarily performed in your own private lodge space, though you may also perform it in other places if you choose. It takes on a further dimension of power and effect when you do it in your own lodge, however, since you are also performing it in the temple that you have been building up in your imagination as you passed through the seven circles.

This is done, as already noted, by visualizing the temple at the beginning of the ceremony, before you open the lodge, and continue to visualize the temple around you as you proceed through the ceremony. The altar of your lodge space becomes the altar in your temple, located in the adytum or sanctuary, and each action of the ceremony is done against the imagined background of the temple you have constructed on the astral plane over the time you have spent working through the previous six circles.

To understand what this does, it is helpful to understand the ancient occult teaching about the macrocosm or "big universe" and the microcosm or "little universe." The first of these is the universe we see around us; the second is the universe within us. Occultists since ancient times have understood that these two reflect each other and affect each other. What happens in the macrocosm affects each individual microcosm, obviously enough, but what happens in each microcosm also has a modest but real effect on the macrocosm.

Occult practices work with the relationship between macrocosm and microcosm in a subtle and powerful way. They do this by establishing a *mesocosm*, a "middle universe" between the macrocosm and the microcosm, which represents both of them. That is what the Sphere of Protection ritual does; it sets up a symbolic model of the universe, which is also a model of yourself, and brings that symbolic model into balance by invoking the elemental powers and banishing those things that need to be banished from yourself and your world. As you practice the Sphere of Protection daily, your actions in the mesocosm of the ritual are reflected outward into the macrocosm and inward into your own microcosm, and bring balance and harmony to both of them.

The lodge opening and closing ceremony you have practiced so many times also establishes a mesocosm and works with it, and so do many of the other practices you have performed while working through the three degrees of the Golden Section Fellowship. The image of your guardian angel or guardian genius that you have been building up during the time you have spent working through this book is also a mesocosm of a different kind: it mediates between your consciousness and a spiritual being who operates on levels of existence you cannot yet perceive. In one way or another, in other words, you have been working with mesocosms through the entire course of your studies in occultism.

The temple you have built up on the astral plane over the months just past, however, is a mesocosm of an especially powerful and useful kind. It exists as a stable structure on the inner planes, established there by your repeated efforts of imagination, but it permits you to work on the inner and outer planes simultaneously. Every time you do ceremonial work while visualizing the temple around you, you help build a bridge between worlds, a point of contact through which the Seen and the Unseen can interact and interpenetrate—that is to say, a temple in the full sense of the word. This allows spiritual forces to flow down into manifestation in matter, and makes it a little easier for souls incarnate on the material plane to proceed upwards in their evolutionary journey toward the realms of spirit.

The mesocosm you have created through your temple visualizations reflects your own microcosm—that is why it has seven windows, corresponding to the seven vortices you have awakened while working through the seven circles of this book. The temple mesocosm also reflects the macrocosm—those same seven windows relate to the seven elemental gates you learned about in *The Way of the Golden Section*, and to many other sevenfold patterns in the cosmos. As you work with it, it will teach you important lessons about the relationship between your microcosm and the macrocosm that surrounds you.

The communion ceremony in group workings

If you have organized a temple of the Golden Section Fellowship according to the instructions given in *The Way of the Four Elements*, you have another option for working with the communion ceremony. While it is not primarily a ritual for a congregation, it may be performed in a temple of that kind as well as in the secret temple you have constructed in the course of working with this book. Among members of the third degree of the Golden Section Fellowship—and *only* among them—the temple in which initiates gather together for ritual work is called an outer temple, while the temple you have constructed on the astral plane is called an inner temple. Keep these terms in mind as we proceed.

The communion ceremony may be enacted any time an outer temple is opened in due form, using the ritual given in *The Way of the Four Elements*. It should be the last thing done before the beginning of the closing ceremony. Only an initiate who has completed the work of *The Way of the Secret Temple* may perform the communion ceremony, but once the bread and wine have been consecrated, any member of the temple may partake of them. As explained earlier, the communion is always taken by intinction: that is, the recipient is given a small piece of bread, dips it in the wine in the chalice, and then puts it in the mouth. When the bread is given to the recipient, the person who has performed the ceremony says, "The bounty of the Earth"; when offering the chalice of wine to the recipient, the words to say are "The glory of the Sun."

It is especially valuable to perform this ceremony as part of the solstice and equinox ceremonies in an outer temple. In those workings, the solar and telluric currents are awakened and called into the temple. The communion ceremony is done immediately after the solstice or equinox ceremony and just before the closing of the temple, and so draws on the potent energies already awakened and present.

Completing the seventh circle

Plan on devoting at least one month to learning and practicing the work of this circle. Before you finish that process, review all the material assigned to the seventh circle and be sure you understand it and have practiced it correctly. Remember that you can always take more time to complete the work if you wish.

When feel you are ready to go on, only one change needs to be made: in the work with the seven vortices, start giving the third eye vortex three breaths rather than seven. Continue practicing the work with the vortices, giving each of them three breaths while spinning them, for the rest of your life. The longer you continue to work with this practice, and the rest of the practices you have learned in your journey through the seven circles, the more benefits you will gain from them.

CHAPTER EIGHT

Beyond the seven circles

Once you have finished studying and practicing the material in the foregoing parts of this book, after first working your way through *The Way of the Golden Section* and *The Way of the Four Elements*, you will have passed through the three degrees and completed the entire core training program of the Golden Section Fellowship. Like your initiation all those months or years ago, this marks the beginning of a journey, not the end of one. You have learned and practiced a great deal, and your task now is to take what you have learned and go forward with it, continuing the Fellowship's quest for wisdom, revelation, and enlightenment.

The first step in that further journey, ironically, involves going back. This is a good time in your studies to review all three of the volumes in this series, to make sure you still remember all the details of the teachings and practices. This is also a good time to read through your practice record from the beginning, assess your work with the various practices, and consider revisiting those you may have neglected.

The basic practices given in this book, alongside those covered in *The Way of the Golden Section*—the Sphere of Protection, the daily meditation session with its various extensions and expansions, and the daily divination—provide a set of occult exercises and workings that you can do each day for the rest of your life, learning, growing, and gaining in wisdom and power all the while. The equinox and solstice rituals you learned in *The Way of the Four Elements,* and the communion ritual included in this book, complete that set of fundamental practices.

What you choose to do with the rest of the material you have learned is up to you at this point. You know how to work with sacred geometry, how to practice scrying and commune with the spirits of the elements, how to use your palm centers to heal and bless, how to fulfill the duties of each of the five minor orders of the Universal Gnostic Church, and more. These things have helped teach you certain lessons about occultism and life. How large or small a role they will play in your future work is up to you.

In the meantime, certain other books may be useful to you in your quest.

Books relevant to the Golden Section Fellowship

The most important of these belong to the Golden Section Fellowship series. This comprises seven volumes in all:

> *The Sacred Geometry Oracle*
> *The Way of the Golden Section*
> *The Way of the Four Elements*
> *The Way of the Secret Temple*
> *The Occult Philosophy Workbook*
> *The Earth Mysteries Workbook*
> *The Life Force Workbook*[17]

By this point you have certainly worked with four of these. The three workbooks are designed to complement the first four volumes; each of them provides a set of lessons, meditations, and other practices that will take one year for you to complete. Unlike the three *Way of …* manuals, the workbooks can be done in any order you prefer.

Certain of my other books also draw on the same tradition of theory and practice that is central to the Golden Section Fellowship:

> *The Dolmen Arch* (two volumes)

These volumes are based on the fragments of a Druid correspondence course circulated in the United States between the two World Wars.

---

[17] As of this writing, this last volume is still in preparation.

Quite a bit of material was missing, so I filled it out with practices and teachings from the Universal Gnostic Church tradition. *The Dolmen Arch* is thus an extensive and detailed course of instruction in Druid occultism, wholly compatible with the material taught by the Golden Section Fellowship.

The Druid Magic Handbook

The first branch of the UGC tradition I explored was the one taught by the Ancient Order of Druids in America (AODA). This book came out of my efforts to expand the AODA system to provide more opportunities for magic and other forms of practical occultism. The Sphere of Protection is the central ritual in this book. It contains formulas of practical magic that can be used by anyone who has studied the Golden Section work.

The Fellowship of the Hermetic Rose (four volumes)

This is my reworking of the rituals and teachings of John Gilbert's Golden Dawn-related magical order.[18] It has been released with a Creative Commons license and so can be downloaded freely from various sites on the internet. It is completely compatible with the Golden Section Fellowship work, and in fact Golden Section initiates will find some aspects of this system very familiar!

Three other books of mine may also be useful:

The Secret of the Five Rites

This volume explores the history and occult dimensions of the Five Rites, a set of physical exercises that work with the same seven vortices you have just awakened.

The Secret of the Temple
The Ceremony of the Grail

My two books (so far!) on the temple tradition mentioned in this volume. These are not practical manuals; they are explorations of the

---

[18] Reworking was necessary because John asked his students to take oaths not to reveal the signs, passwords, and a few other details of his system. I replaced these with equivalents that work equally well.

hidden history of the world, tracing forgotten traditions and secret initiatory practices from ancient times to the dawn of the modern world. *The Ceremony of the Grail*, however, also contains my reconstruction of the original ceremony of initiation around which the legends of the Holy Grail took shape. This can be performed with good results in a temple of the Golden Section Fellowship, and the initiation itself—a ceremony meant to bring the candidate into closer contact with the One Life—is worth experiencing.

Other resources

Of course, my books are far from the only resources that may be of use to you in your ongoing quest for wisdom, revelation, and enlightenment. The occult traditions of the Western world have produced bumper crops of books down through the years. While some of these are of very uneven quality, others have earned a reputation as classics. The occult writings of Dion Fortune, Manly P. Hall, and Gareth Knight are particularly recommended. Another writer worth studying is John Michell; his works are not always historically accurate, but he had a profound grasp of sacred geometry and occult tradition. Read his books as inspired poetry rather than as textbooks and they have much to teach.

As of this writing, additionally, four of the orders that were once part of the Universal Gnostic Church tradition are active again, and have teachings worth studying. The Ancient Order of Druids in America (website: aoda.org) is one of the largest and most active Druid orders in North America today; the Order of Spiritual Alchemy (website: octagonsociety.org) is smaller and quieter, but continues to teach its distinctive system of emotional and mental healing. The Modern Order of Essenes exists as a network of individual Essene Master Teachers; as yet it has no website, but its teachers and healers can be found online in various venues. The Fellowship of the Hermetic Rose likewise exists as a loose network of practitioners who study and practice the material I have put into circulation. The Universal Gnostic Church itself is still dormant—but that may change; as of this writing, several people have begun the demanding process of preparing themselves to qualify for priesthood or priestesshood in the UGC.

One way or another, whatever path you take in your quest, whatever resources you use in your personal search for wisdom, revelation, and enlightenment, know that my blessing goes with you if you desire it.

—John Michael Greer

APPENDIX

Practices of the golden section fellowship

The occult disciplines taught in this book do not stand alone. They are meant to serve as a third, more advanced level of practice, following on after the basic practices covered in *The Way of the Golden Section* and the intermediate practices given in *The Way of the Four Elements*. The following practices are given here for the convenience of students of the work, so that they can look up unfamiliar details without having to fumble with multiple books.

Please keep in mind, however, that no occult practice can ever really be mastered until it is committed to memory and practiced without looking up details. The daily practices assigned to initiates of the Golden Section Fellowship should be memorized and mastered first, before taking on the further levels of practice covered earlier in this book.

The Sphere of Protection

The Sphere of Protection ritual is the basic ritual practice of the Golden Section Fellowship. It is learned in stages, as described in *The Way of the Golden Section* (and in another form, in *The Druid Magic Handbook* and *The Dolmen Arch*).

Lodge version

First, stand in the center of your lodge, facing your altar. Sweep your arms up to your sides until your hands meet above your head. Join then with the fingers of the right hand at right angles across the fingers of the left. Draw your joined hands down to your forehead, and touch with them the point between your eyebrows, at the location of your third eye center; as you do this, imagine a beam of pure white light descending from infinite space to a point in the center of your head, forming a small sphere of light there. Say "By the sky above me" (or the first phrase of another invocation you have chosen). Draw the hands down to your abdomen and send the beam of light to the center of the earth, and say, "By the earth beneath me" (or the second phase of your invocation). Sweep your hands up, out, and down to your sides, imagining the light returning from the center of the earth and fountaining out through the crown of your head to fill the area around you; say "By the life within me" (or the third phrase of your invocation). Cross your hands over your chest, right arm over left, and say, "May this lodge be blessed and guarded now and always" (or the fourth phrase of your invocation). This completes the opening.

Second, face East and trace the Sign of Air clockwise, visualizing it in yellow light and saying these words:

> By the yellow gate of the rushing winds and the hawk of May in the heights of morning, I invoke the Air and all its powers. May the powers of Air bless and protect this lodge this day and always, and further its work.

When you have contemplated Air for a time, say, "I thank the powers of Air for their gifts." Then trace the Sign of Air counterclockwise, saying these words: "And with the help of the powers of Air, I banish from within and around this lodge all harmful and disturbing influences and every imbalance of the nature of Air. I banish these far from this place."

Third, face South and trace the Sign of Fire clockwise, visualizing it in red light and saying these words:

> By the red gate of the bright flames and the white stag of the summer greenwood, I invoke the Fire and all its powers. May the powers of Fire bless and protect this lodge this day and always, and further its work.

When you have contemplated Fire for a time, say, "I thank the powers of Fire for their gifts." Then trace the Sign of Fire counterclockwise, saying these words: "And with the help of the powers of Fire, I banish from within and around this lodge all harmful and disturbing influences and every imbalance of the nature of Fire. I banish these far from this place."

Fourth, face West and trace the Sign of Water clockwise, visualizing it in blue light and saying these words:

> By the blue gate of the mighty waters and the salmon of wisdom in the sacred pool, I invoke the Water and all its powers. May the powers of Water bless and protect this lodge this day and always, and further its work.

When you have contemplated Water for a time, say, "I thank the powers of Water for their gifts." Then trace the Sign of Water counterclockwise, saying these words: "And with the help of the powers of Water, I banish from within and around this lodge all harmful and disturbing influence and every imbalance of the nature of Water. I banish these far from this place."

Fifth, face North and trace the Sign of Earth clockwise, visualizing it in green light and saying these words:

> By the green gate of the tall stones and the great bear of the starry heavens, I invoke the Earth and all its powers. May the powers of Earth bless and protect this lodge this day and always, and further its work.

When you have contemplated Earth for a time, say, "I thank the powers of Earth for their gifts." Then trace the Sign of Earth counterclockwise, saying these words: "And with the help of the powers of Earth, I banish from within and around this lodge all harmful and disturbing influences and every imbalance of the nature of Earth. I banish these far from this place."

Sixth, point down and trace the Sign of Spirit Below, visualizing it in orange light. Then send it down into the earth, saying these words:

> By the orange gate of Spirit Below and the power of the telluric current, I invoke Spirit Below and all its powers. May the powers of Spirit Below bless and protect this lodge this day and always, and further its work.

Sense the power of Spirit Below blessing the lodge, and say, "I thank the powers of Spirit Below for their gifts."

Seventh, point up and trace the Sign of Spirit Above, visualizing it in purple light. Then send it up into the sky, saying:

> By the purple gate of Spirit Above and the power of the solar current, I invoke Spirit Above and all its powers. May the powers of Spirit Above bless and protect this lodge this day and always, and further its work.

Sense the power of Spirit Above blessing the lodge, and say, "I thank the powers of Spirit Above for their gifts."

Eighth, be aware of all six Signs around you and then of yourself in the midst of them. Say:

> By the six powers here invoked and here present and the secret of the lunar current, and in the Grand Word AWEN, I invoke Spirit Within. May the powers of Spirit Within me bless and protect this lodge this day and always, and further its work. May they establish about this lodge a Sphere of Protection.

Turn your attention to your solar plexus. Imagine a small sphere of light there, and imagine it expanding. It grows until it surrounds your entire body, and as much further as you need to make it to encompass the area you wish to place within its protection. Concentrate, as it expands, on the sense that the space inside it is lighter, cleaner, and brighter than the space outside it. Pause and feel the space around you as cleansed, lightened, and illuminated. Then cross your arms as you did at the end of the opening, and say "May the powers of Nature bless and protect this lodge this day and always." This completes the Sphere of Protection.

Individual version

The ritual for daily practice by initiates of the Golden Section Fellowship is somewhat different, and incorporates the awakening of the solar plexus and pineal centers discussed earlier in this book. It is performed as follows:

First, perform the opening exactly as described above.

APPENDIX 115

Second, invoke Air in the East in the usual way, saying these words:

> By the yellow gate of the rushing winds and the hawk of May in the heights of morning, I invoke the Air and all its powers. May the powers of Air bless and protect me this day and always, and further my work. May they help me attain helpful attitudes and true insights.

When you have contemplated Air for a time, say, "I thank the powers of Air for their gifts." Then banish with Air in the usual way, saying these words:

> And with the help of the powers of Air, I banish from within me and around me and from all my doings all harmful influences and hostile magic, all negative habits of mind, and every imbalance of the nature of Air. I banish these far from me.

Third, invoke Fire in the South in the usual way, saying these words:

> By the red gate of the bright flames and the white stag of the summer greenwood, I invoke the Fire and all its powers. May the powers of Fire bless and protect me this day and always, and further my work. May they help me attain reasonable desires and wise decisions.

When you have contemplated Fire for a time, say, "I thank the powers of Fire for their gifts." Then banish with Fire in the usual way, saying these words:

> And with the help of the powers of Fire, I banish from within me and around me and from all my doings all harmful influences and hostile magic, all negative habits of will, and every imbalance of the nature of Fire. I banish these far from me.

Fourth, invoke Water in the West in the usual way, saying these words:

> By the blue gate of the mighty waters and the salmon of wisdom in the sacred pool, I invoke the Water and all its powers. May the powers of Water bless and protect me this day and always, and

further my work. May they help me attain helpful relationships and balanced emotions.

When you have contemplated Water for a time, say, "I thank the powers of Water for their gifts." Then banish with Water in the usual way, saying these words:

> And with the help of the powers of Water, I banish from within me and around me and from all my doings all harmful influences and hostile magic, all negative habits of emotion, and every imbalance of the nature of Water. I banish these far from me.

Fifth, invoke Earth in the North in the usual way, saying these words:

> By the green gate of the tall stones and the great bear of the starry heavens, I invoke the Earth and all its powers. May the powers of Earth bless and protect me this day and always, and further my work. May they help me attain robust health and provide for my material needs.

When you have contemplated Earth for a time, say, "I thank the powers of Earth for their gifts." Then banish with Earth in the usual way, saying these words:

> And with the help of the powers of Earth, I banish from within me and around me and from all my doings all harmful influences and hostile magic, all negative habits of body, and every imbalance of the nature of Earth. I banish these far from me.

Sixth, invoke Spirit Below in the usual way, saying these words:

> By the orange gate of Spirit Below and the power of the telluric current, I invoke Spirit Below and all its powers. May the powers of Spirit Below bless and protect me this day and always, and further my work. May the telluric current arise and fill me with life.

Breathe in a slow deep breath, and as you do so, imagine the telluric current bubbling up through the soles of your feet like cool, sparkling spring water. Imagine it flowing up into your entire body, filling it with a feeling of vitality. As you breathe out, feel the current remaining in your body, and say, "I thank the powers of Spirit Below for their gifts."

Seventh, invoke Spirit Above in the usual way, saying:

> By the purple gate of Spirit Above and the power of the solar current, I invoke Spirit Above and all its powers. May the powers of Spirit Above bless and protect me this day and always, and further my work. May the solar current descend and fill me with light.

Breathe in a slow deep breath, and as you do so, imagine the solar current streaming down through the top of your head like clear bright sunlight. Imagine it flowing down into your entire body, filling it with a feeling of lightness and brightness. As you breathe out, feel the current remaining in your body, and say, "I thank the powers of Spirit Above for their gifts."

Eighth, invoke Spirit Within in the usual way, saying:

> By the six powers here invoked and here present and the secret of the lunar current, and in the Grand Word AWEN, I invoke Spirit Within. May the powers of Spirit Within me bless and protect me this day and always, and further my work. May the lunar current be born in me and kindle the Inner Flame.

As you breathe in, imagine the energies of the solar and telluric currents inside you drawing together into your solar plexus and becoming a golden sphere of light, like a little sun a few inches across. As you breathe out, imagine a slender line of light rising up from the solar plexus along the midline of your body to the center of your head, where it kindles a little flame like the flame of a candle, but the pure white color of starlight. Repeat this two more times, drawing the energies together into an inner sun on the in-breath and sending a line of light up to the center of your head on the out-breath.

Ninth, say: "By that flame, and with the help of all the powers I have invoked, I establish about myself a Sphere of Protection." Then perform the closing visualization in the same way as before. This completes the initiate's Sphere of Protection.

Discursive meditation

The method of meditation used by the Golden Section Fellowship, and by most traditional Western occult schools, differs in an important way from the Eastern methods of meditation commonly practiced these days. Although there are exceptions, most Eastern methods of meditation work by turning off the objective mind—that is, the ordinary conscious mind. The core traditions of Western meditation, by contrast, direct the focus of the objective mind on thinking itself, and turn the objective mind into a vehicle for spiritual awareness. In the standard Western method of meditation, this is done by focusing the mind on a specific topic, called a *theme*, and mentally following out the implications of that theme through a chain of ideas, all the while keeping the objective mind focused on the theme. With practice, the deeper, subjective mind joins in, and begins to hand the objective mind ideas and insights it wouldn't otherwise have had, so that meditation becomes a way for your two minds to work together.

This form of meditation is called *discursive meditation*, because it often takes the form of an inner discourse or dialogue. To practice it, you will need a place that is quiet and not too brightly lit. It should be private—a room with a door you can shut is best, though if you can't arrange that, a quiet corner and a little forbearance on the part of your housemates will do the job. You'll need a chair with a straight back, and a seat at a height that allows you to rest your feet flat on the floor while keeping your thighs level with the ground. You'll need a clock or watch, placed so that you can see it easily without moving your head. Once you have these simple preliminaries in place you are ready to begin.

Posture

One of the benefits of discursive meditation is that you don't have to tie your legs into a knot to practice it. The posture to use is the one shown in any Egyptian statue of a seated god or goddess. Sit on a relatively hard chair. If it has a back, slide forward, so your back doesn't touch the chair's back at all. Your feet should rest flat on the floor, your knees and hips are at right angles, your hands rest palm down on your thighs, and your head is straight. Keep your eyes open but relax your eyelids; look forward and down, as though at something on the floor a few yards ahead of you. Breathe slowly and easily.

Relaxation

The practice of sitting in a fixed and slightly unnatural posture is meant to keep you from being too relaxed. Keeping the spine straight, the head held up, the legs parallel, and the body still requires tension. Now we move to the other side of the balance and make sure you aren't too tense. This is done by relaxing your muscles while retaining the posture you've established. You don't move at all; you don't shift or wiggle or stretch; you just let go of the tensions you don't need to keep the posture.

Start at the crown of the head, Consciously relax any muscular tensions you find there. If you encounter a tension that won't let go, imagine that it is relaxing. (Your subjective mind will notice this, and the imagination will become reality with a little practice.) Spend a little while on that part of your body, and then move further down your head to the sides of the skull. Consciously relax any tensions you find there, if you can, and if you can't, imagine the tensions dissolving. Go all the way down your whole body this way, taking it a bit at a time, and doing the same twofold relaxation on each part of your body—consciously relax what you can, and imagine the rest letting go. This should take you at least five minutes, and quite possibly more than that. All the while, maintain the seated posture without moving. Don't pay attention to your breath—that's a later phase—or to anything outside yourself; simply focus on your body, and on the process by which you're releasing unnecessary tensions.

Breathing

How you breathe has powerful effects on your state of consciousness, and there are intricate systems of breathwork that take advantage of this for various purposes. If you don't have a teacher to supervise you and watch for signs of trouble, though, those can be risky. Breathwork stimulates the vagus nerve, a nerve that connects the vital organs with the brain, and so has a range of effects on your nervous system and your glands; if you do intensive breathwork without supervision, as a result, you can give yourself health problems.

Fortunately there are methods of breathwork that are safe to practice on your own, and one of them is very commonly used in occult meditation. It's called the Fourfold Breath. It's quite simple. You breathe in through your nose, slowly and deeply, to the count of four. You hold the breath in for the count of four. You breathe out through your nose, slowly and fully, to the count of four. You hold the breath out to the count of four. Repeat to the same steady rhythm.

How do you know how slow or fast to make the rhythm? Simply make it reasonably slow, but not so slow that you gasp or run out of air. Keep the movement of your breath steady, gentle, and flowing. No two people will have exactly the same rhythm, nor will you have the same rhythm every time you practice. Don't use a metronome or any other mechanical aid; just let yourself find a pace that works for you.

Meditation

When you're ready to begin meditation, set up the diagram for the lesson you're studying so you can see it clearly from your meditation chair without turning your head. Sit down in the position we've discussed and settle into it, neither tense nor relaxed but poised. Let go of excess tension, beginning from the top of your head and letting it drain down from there; spend about a minute at that. Then do five minutes of the Fourfold Breath, letting your mind focus solely on your breathing. At this point you're ready to begin.

Spend a few moments considering the theme of the meditation. Recall it as clearly as you can. Hold it in your mind for a little while, considering it as though you were looking at a material object, and then begin thinking about it.

As you do so, your thoughts will wander off the theme. Bring them back. They'll wander off again. Bring them back again. You'll have as much trouble keeping your mind on the theme as the practitioner of mind-emptying styles of meditation has keeping thoughts at bay, and you'll develop the same skills of catching your mind wandering and bringing it back to the subject of the meditation. In the intervals between these vagaries, on the other hand, you'll be learning something about the theme, and you'll also be working on the capacity for focused reflective thought, an essential human skill and one very poorly developed by most of us in the present age of the world. Meditate on the theme you have chosen for at least ten minutes, and as much more as seems useful to you. When you are finished, take a deep breath or two and then go on with the rest of your day.

Meditation is best practiced in a space that has been cleared and cleansed by the Sphere of Protection or by some other banishing ritual, such as the Lesser Banishing Ritual of the Pentagram. A banishing ritual followed by a session of discursive meditation makes a fine daily practice for any occultist, and will develop the inner abilities needed to go further in occultism.

Lodge ceremonies

A lodge of the Golden Section Fellowship is a personal working space, the place where each initiate performs his or her daily practices and other occult exercises. As explained in *The Way of the Golden Section*, it requires no complicated setting: a spare corner of a room with a chair and a flat surface to use as an altar is quite adequate. The ceremonies used to open and close a lodge, which are used in the equinox and solstice ceremonies and also to consecrate the elemental working tools, are as follows.

Lodge opening ceremony

The opening ceremony for a lodge of the Golden Section Fellowship is done as follows:

First, stand in your lodge in front of the chair, facing the altar, with incense burning in the central cauldron. Pause for a moment and clear your mind, then say aloud, "May the powers of Nature assist me to open this lodge of the Golden Section Fellowship in due form. Let peace first be proclaimed to the four quarters."

Second, face East and raise your right hand with the palm outward in salute. Say, "May there be peace in the East." Turn to face South, raise your hand in the same way, saying, "May there be peace in the South." Turn to face West and repeat the gesture, saying, "May there be peace in the West." Turn to the North, repeat the gesture, and say, "May there be peace in the North." As you do each of these, imagine peace and harmony flowing outward from your lodge to bless the four quarters of the world.

Third, face the altar again and say, "Since peace has been proclaimed, let this lodge be established, purified, and consecrated with the Three Principles."

122 APPENDIX

Fourth, go to the altar, pick up the cauldron of salt, and raise it up as though in offering. Then bring it back down to somewhere around the level of your solar plexus.

You are now going to use the cauldron of salt to establish the boundaries of your lodge, by drawing a square around the lodge with it going clockwise, as shown in the diagram below. Hold the cauldron in your left hand and go to your right, drawing a straight line from the altar to the corner of your lodge (which does not have to be the corner of the room). Make a right angle, and trace one side of the square; make another right angle, and trace another; make another and trace the third, and then a fourth right angle and another movement should bring you back to the altar and complete the square, as shown in the diagram. As you do this, imagine the cauldron drawing a line in emerald-green light.

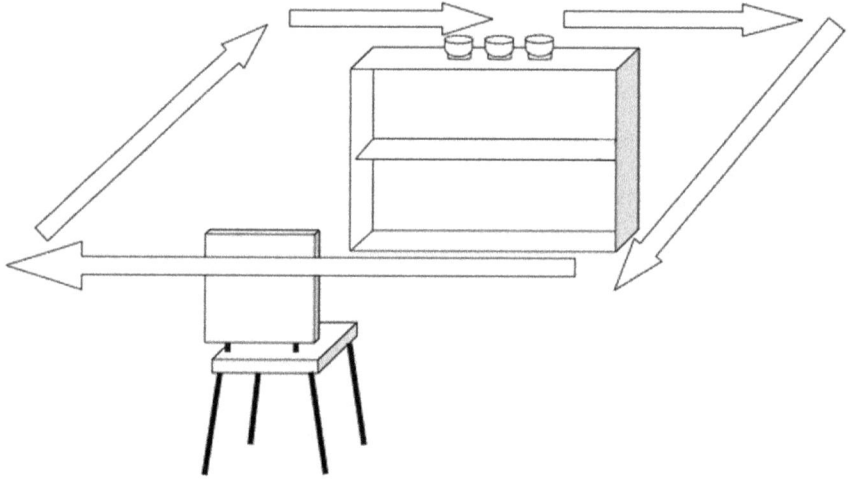

Opening ritual 1

Fifth, put the cauldron of salt back in its place and pick up the cauldron of water. Raise it as though in offering, and then bring it back down to around solar plexus level. Now go around the lodge again, using the cauldron of water to draw a triangle surrounding the lodge, as shown in the first diagram on the next page. As you do this, imagine the cauldron drawing a line in sky-blue light.

APPENDIX 123

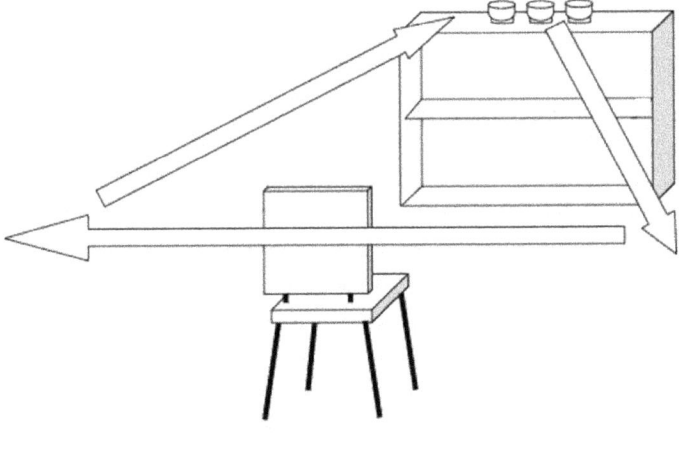

Opening ritual 2

Sixth, put the cauldron of water back in its place and pick up the cauldron of incense. Raise it as though in offering and bring it back down to solar plexus level. Now go around the lodge a third time, using the cauldron to draw a circle surrounding the lodge, as shown in the diagram below. As you do this, imagine the cauldron drawing a line in pure white light.

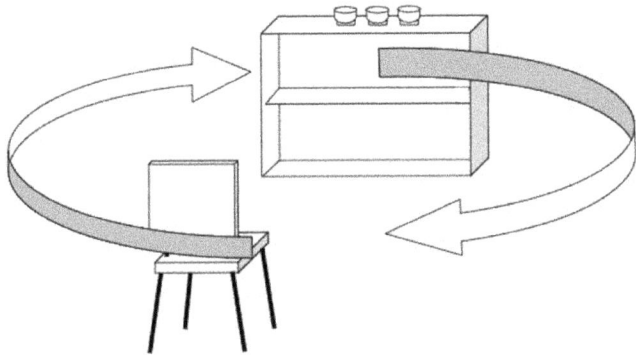

Opening ritual 3

Put the cauldron of incense back in its place. The result of these movements, of course, is that you have drawn the Outer Emblem of the

Fellowship in the space surrounding your chair and the working area of your lodge, as shown from above in the diagram below.

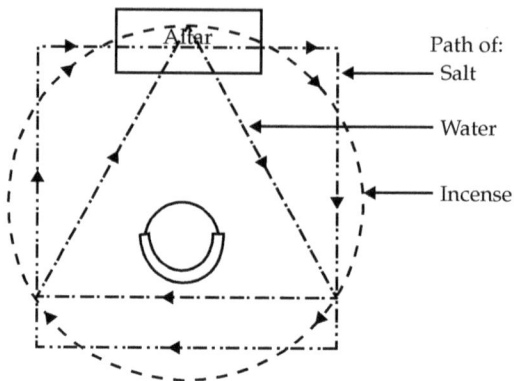

Completed opening ritual

Seventh, stand in front of the chair again, and say aloud, "Let a Sphere of Protection now be formulated." Then perform the complete Sphere of Protection ritual. This is done in the same way you've learned already, but with one difference: you are placing the Sphere of Protection about your lodge rather than yourself. When you invoke the element of Air, for example, you say:

> By the yellow gate of the rushing winds and the hawk of May in the heights of morning, I invoke the Air and all its powers. May the powers of Air bless and protect this lodge this day and always, and further its work.

Then, after thanking the powers of Air and tracing the symbol counterclockwise: "And with the help of the powers of Air, I banish from within and around this lodge all harmful influences and hostile magic and every imbalance of the nature of Air. I banish them far from this place." Change the words in the same way for each of the other six phases, and make sure the sphere of light at the closing phase extends out beyond the square, triangle, and circle you have traced around the lodge.

Eighth, when you have completed the Sphere of Protection, go to the altar. Put the straightedge in front of the central cauldron, open the compasses, and lay them atop the straightedge, in the form shown in Straightedge and compasses below, with the handle of the compass pointing away from you. This represents the Three Rays of Light that, according to the symbolism of the Druid Revival, brought the world into being.

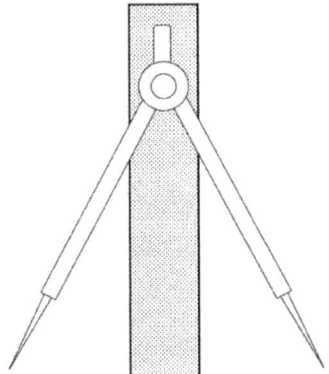

Straightedge and compasses

Ninth, step back and stand in front of the chair. Say the following: "With the help of the powers of Nature and in the name and the presence of the eternal Spiritual Sun, I declare this lodge of the Golden Section Fellowship open in due form." As you say this, imagine the Sun high above the lodge, shining its rays down onto you. Hold this image for a while, and then sit down. This completes the opening ceremony, and you can now go on to the work of the lodge.

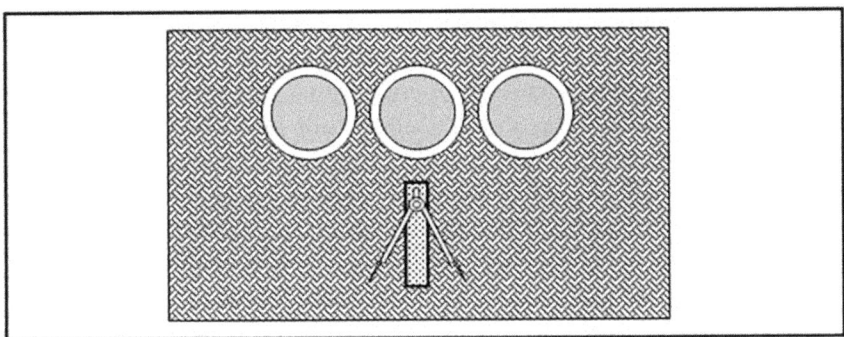

Altar diagram 1

Lodge closing ceremony

Whenever you have performed the opening ceremony, you should perform the closing ceremony before you return to ordinary activities. The closing ceremony is done as follows.

First, stand up, facing the altar. Pause for a moment and clear your mind, then say aloud, "May the powers of Nature assist me to close this lodge of the Golden Section Fellowship in due form. Let the quarters again be acknowledged."

Second, salute the East as you did in the opening, but this time say: "May peace abide in the East." Do the same thing in the South, West, and North, changing the words appropriately.

Third, face the altar again and say: "Since peace has again been proclaimed, let the lodge be unwoven and the Three Principles returned to their sources." You will now unwind and erase the pattern of subtle influences you created in the opening ceremony, using the cauldrons as before.

Fourth, go to the altar, pick up the cauldron of incense, and walk with it in a circle, going counterclockwise around the lodge. (This is the reverse of the movement shown in the diagram Opening ritual 3.) As you do this, imagine the cauldron absorbing and erasing the line of white light it drew in the opening. When you have finished and brought the cauldron back to the altar, raise it up as in salute, and then put it back in its place on the altar.

Fifth, pick up the cauldron of water, and proceed with it in a triangular pattern around the lodge, going counterclockwise. (This is the reverse of the movement shown in the diagram Opening ritual 2.) As you do this, imagine the cauldron absorbing and erasing the line of blue light it drew in the opening. When you have finished and brought the cauldron back to the altar, raise it up as in salute, and then put it back in its place on the altar.

Sixth, pick up the cauldron of salt, and proceed with it in a square pattern around the lodge, going counterclockwise. (This is the reverse of the movement shown in the diagram Opening ritual 1.) As you do this, imagine the cauldron absorbing and erasing the line of green light it drew in the opening. When you have finished and brought the cauldron back to the altar, raise it up as in salute, and then put it back in its place on the altar.

Seventh, step back from the altar to stand in front of the chair, facing the altar, and say: "Let any energies awakened in this working not needed to fulfill its purpose be returned to the Earth for her blessing." Imagine the subtle energies you have called into the lodge flowing down from the lodge to the heart of the Earth. Maintain the visualization for several minutes, or until the lodge room feels clear.

Eighth, imagine a golden Sun high above the lodge, with rays streaming down. Say these words: "May all beings join in the contemplation. Let us contemplate the Light of Lights, the Sun of Suns, the unquenched flame within each living soul." Then, imagining every being in all the universe joining in these words: "May we receive enlightenment from that great Source."

Ninth, go to the altar. Close the compass and put it back in its place, and then put the straightedge back in its place. Then step back to stand in front of your chair and say: "With the help of the powers of Nature, I declare this lodge of the Golden Section Fellowship closed in due form." This completes the closing ceremony.

Spring equinox ceremony

This ritual should be performed within 48 hours at most of the moment of the equinox, which you can find online or in any almanac. As discussed earlier, it marks the end of the previous phase of elemental work and the beginning of your initiation into the mysteries of Air. It is performed as follows.

First, prepare the materials for the communion ceremony, and then open with the opening ceremony.

Second, speak aloud the following words.

> The Spring Equinox has arrived, and the Sun and Earth renew the bonds that unite them. In this time of balanced powers, I invoke the blessings of the powers of Nature upon myself, the Golden Section Fellowship, and the Earth.
>
> In the world of Nature, the winter has ended and the Sun has completed half its long journey toward the North. The streams are full of water from the melting snow and the spring rains; sap rises in the trees and flowers begin to bloom. Birds return from their winter dwellings far to the South as life wakes from its time of sleep.
>
> The ancients knew this season as the seedtime of the year, not only for the farmer and the herder but also for those who stand at the gates between the Seen and the Unseen. They recognized at this time the power of the thought held in the mind's clarity and the word spoken upon the wind's breath; they called down wisdom from the Sun and called up power from the Earth to illuminate their minds.
>
> Therefore the work of this season begins from the quarter of Air.

Third, face East. Visualize the presence of the elements of Air and Water in their quarters, and feel the polarity between them. Say: "East; West. Air; Water. The realm of the Mind; the realm of the Heart. May they enter into the great harmony."

Fourth, visualize the presence of the elements of Fire and Earth in their quarters, and feel the polarity between them. Say: "South; North. Fire; Earth. The realm of the Spirit; the realm of the Body. May they enter into the great harmony."

Fifth, visualize the presence of all four elements in their quarters, and feel the complex fourfold relationship among them. Say: "The realm of the Winds; the realm of the Flames; the realm of the Waves; the realm of the Stones. May they enter into the great harmony."

Sixth, say: "By the hawk of May in the heights of morning, I invoke the Air and the powers of the Air! May their blessings be with all beings during the season to come." While saying this, imagine a blazing star at the zenith, almost infinitely far above the lodge; this is Fomalhaut, the Royal Star governing the ceremony.

Seventh, face South, and say: "By the white stag of the summer greenwood, I invoke the Fire and the powers of the Fire! May their blessings be with all beings during the season to come." While saying this, imagine a ray of light descending from the star at infinite height to the golden sphere of the Sun, blazing at zenith above the lodge, high above but much closer than the star.

Eighth, face West, and say: "By the salmon of wisdom who dwells in the sacred pool, I invoke the Water and the powers of the Water! May their blessings be with all beings during the season to come." While saying this, imagine the ray of light descending further from the blazing Sun to the sphere of the full Moon standing at the zenith above the lodge, high above but much closer than the Sun.

Ninth, face North, and say: "By the great bear who guards the starry heavens, I invoke the Earth and the powers of the Earth! May their blessings be with all beings during the season to come." While saying this, imagine the ray of light descending from the shining Moon all the way to the Sphere of Protection you established around the lodge. The entire Sphere is seen to be filled with rainbow-colored light, which radiates outward in all directions.

Tenth, face the altar. Say: "In this season of spring may the Sun send forth his rays of blessing; may the Earth receive that blessing and bring forth her abundance."

Eleventh, go to the altar and prepare it for the communion ceremony. Then proceed with the communion ceremony as explained earlier in this book.

Twelfth, be seated and enter into meditation, taking the season of spring as your theme. When you have meditated for a time, cast a divination using the Sacred Geometry Oracle or any other divinatory method you prefer, and take it as a guide for your work during the season ahead. Perform the closing ritual to finish.

Summer solstice ceremony

This ritual should be performed within 48 hours at most of the moment of the solstice, which you can find online or in any almanac. As discussed earlier, it marks the end of the previous phase of elemental work and the beginning of your initiation into the mysteries of Fire. It is performed as follows.

First, prepare the materials for the communion ceremony, and then open with the opening ceremony.

Second, speak aloud the following words.

> The Summer Solstice has arrived, and the Sun and Earth manifest the polarities of being. In this time of balanced powers, I invoke the blessings of the powers of Nature upon myself, the Golden Section Fellowship, and the Earth.
>
> In the world of Nature, spring's promise has given way to summer's fulfillment and the Sun now stands at its highest point in the sky, preparing for its long journey into darkness. The land is mantled in green as every growing thing bends its strength toward the harvest. Life rejoices in the golden afternoon of the year even as it makes its preparations for the cold months to come.
>
> The ancients knew this season as the year's bright summit, and waited in their temples for the fiery sign of midsummer sunrise, the seal of harmony that unites the turning worlds. They recognized at this time the power of destiny born from the innermost self and the kindling flame of the awakening spirit; they turned their faces to the Sun and set their feet upon the Earth to accomplish the work of their wills.
>
> Therefore the work of this season begins from the quarter of Fire.

Third, face South. Visualize the presence of the elements of Earth and Fire in their quarters, and feel the polarity between them. Say: "South; North. Fire; Earth. The realm of the Spirit; the realm of the Body. May they enter into the great harmony."

Fourth, visualize the presence of the elements of Water and Air in their quarters, and feel the polarity between them. Say: "East; West. Air; Water. The realm of the Mind; the realm of the Heart: May they enter into the great harmony."

Fifth, visualize the presence of all four elements in their quarters, and feel the complex fourfold relationship among them. Say: "The realm of the Flames; the realm of the Waves; the realm of the Stones; the realm of the Winds. May they enter into the great harmony."

Sixth, face East. Say: "By the hawk of May in the heights of morning, I invoke the Air and the powers of the Air! May their blessings be with all beings during the season to come." While saying this, imagine a blazing star at the zenith, almost infinitely far above the lodge; this is Aldebaran, the Royal Star governing the ceremony.

Seventh, face South. Say: "By the white stag of the summer greenwood, I invoke the Fire and the powers of the Fire! May their blessings be with all beings during the season to come." While saying this, imagine a ray of light descending from the star at infinite height to the golden sphere of the Sun, blazing at zenith above the lodge, high above but much closer than the star.

Eighth, face West. Say: "By the salmon of wisdom who dwells in the sacred pool, I invoke the Water and the powers of the Water! May their blessings be with all beings during the season to come." While saying this, imagine the ray of light descending further from the blazing Sun to the sphere of the full Moon standing at the zenith above the lodge, high above but much closer than the Sun.

Ninth, face North. Say: "By the great bear who guards the starry heavens, I invoke the Earth and the powers of the Earth! May their blessings be with all beings during the season to come." While saying this, imagine the ray of light descending from the shining Moon all the way to the Sphere of Protection you established around the lodge. The entire Sphere is seen to be filled with rainbow-colored light, which radiates outward in all directions.

Tenth, face the altar and say: "In this season of summer may the Sun make manifest the power of Light. May the Earth reflect that manifestation in the power of Life."

Eleventh, go to the altar and prepare it for the communion ceremony. Then proceed with the communion ceremony as explained earlier in this book.

Twelfth, be seated and enter into meditation, taking the season of summer as your theme. When you have meditated for a time, cast a divination using the Sacred Geometry Oracle or any other divinatory method you prefer, and take it as a guide for your work during the season ahead. Perform the closing ritual to finish.

Autumn equinox ceremony

This ritual should be performed within 48 hours at most of the moment of the equinox, which you can find online or in any almanac. As discussed earlier, it marks the end of the previous phase of elemental work and the beginning of your initiation into the mysteries of Water. It is performed as follows.

First, prepare the materials for the communion ceremony, and then open with the opening ceremony.

Second, speak aloud the following words.

> The Autumn Equinox has arrived, and the Sun and Earth renew the bonds that unite them. In this time of balanced powers, I invoke the blessings of the powers of Nature upon myself, the Golden Section Fellowship, and the Earth.
>
> In the world of Nature, summer has given way and the Sun sinks from the heights of heaven into the South. The leaves of the trees blaze with orange and red as the fields turn harvest gold. The cries of the geese sound overhead as they begin their long journey toward their winter homes. Squirrels leap from branch to branch as they prepare for the long cold months to come; the sound of clashing antlers rings through the woods as stags test their strength before the watchful eyes of does.
>
> The ancients knew this season as the harvest time of the year, not only for those who gathered in the sheaves and led the cattle down from summer pastures but also for the wise whose harvest is the lore of past ages and the whispers of the Unseen. They recognized at this time the power of the desire cherished in the heart's silence and the bonds that reach from person to person like the sea uniting shore with shore; they called down power from

the Sun and called up wisdom from the Earth to illuminate their hearts.

Therefore the work of this season begins from the quarter of Water.

Third, face West. Say the following words, visualizing the presence of the elements of Air and Water in their quarters, and feeling the polarity between them: "West; East. Water; Air. The realm of the Heart; the realm of the Mind. May they enter into the great harmony."

Fourth, say the following words, visualizing the presence of the elements of Fire and Earth in their quarters, and feeling the polarity between them: "North; South. Earth; Fire. The realm of the Body; the realm of the Spirit. May they enter into the great harmony."

Fifth, visualize the presence of all four elements in their quarters, and feel the complex fourfold relationship among them. Say: "The realm of the Waves; the realm of the Stones; the realm of the Winds; the realm of the Flames. May they enter into the great harmony."

Sixth, face East and say: "By the hawk of May in the heights of morning, I invoke the Air and the powers of the Air! May their blessings be with all beings during the season to come." As you say this, imagine a blazing star at the zenith, almost infinitely far above the lodge; this is Regulus, the Royal Star governing the ceremony.

Seventh, face South and say: "By the white stag of the summer greenwood, I invoke the Fire and the powers of the Fire! May their blessings be with all beings during the season to come." As you say this, imagine a ray of light descending from the star to the golden sphere of the Sun, blazing at zenith above the lodge, high above but much closer than the star.

Eighth, face West and say: "By the salmon of wisdom who dwells in the sacred pool, I invoke the Water and the powers of the Water! May their blessings be with all beings during the season to come." As you say this, imagine the ray of light descending further to the sphere of the full Moon standing at the zenith above the lodge, high above but much closer than the Sun.

Ninth, face North and say: "By the great bear who guards the starry heavens, I invoke the Earth and the powers of the Earth! May their blessings be with all beings during the season to come." As you say this, imagine the ray of light descending from the shining Moon all the way to the Sphere of Protection you established around the lodge. The entire

Sphere is seen to be filled with rainbow-colored light, which radiates outward in all directions.

Face the altar, and say: "In this season of autumn may the Sun send forth his rays of blessing; may the Earth receive that blessing and bring forth her abundance."

Eleventh, go to the altar and prepare it for the communion ceremony. Then proceed with the communion ceremony as explained earlier in this book.

Twelfth, be seated and enter into meditation, taking the season of spring as your theme. When you have meditated for a time, cast a divination using the Sacred Geometry Oracle or any other divinatory method you prefer, and take it as a guide for your work during the season ahead. Perform the closing ritual to finish.

Winter solstice ceremony

This ritual should be performed within 48 hours at most of the moment of the solstice, which you can find online or in any almanac. As discussed earlier, it marks the end of the previous phase of elemental work and the beginning of your initiation into the mysteries of Earth. It is performed as follows.

First, prepare the materials for the communion ceremony, and then open with the opening ceremony.

Second, speak aloud the following words:

> The Winter Solstice has arrived, and the Sun and Earth manifest the polarities of being. In this time of balanced powers, I invoke the blessings of the powers of Nature upon myself, the Golden Section Fellowship, and the Earth.
>
> In the world of nature, the harvest is over and the Sun has descended to the place of his death and rebirth. Cold blows the wind, and colder still lie the snow and the bare earth and the bare black branches of the trees beneath the bright stars; ice rimes the edges of the streams and breath bursts white from the lips. Only those creatures that cannot sleep the winter away pace through the silence of the cold days and wait for the coming of spring.
>
> The ancients knew this season as the end and beginning of the year, and waited in their temples for the first light of the newborn Sun, the promise of the new year yet to come. They recognized

at this time the power of patience and the wisdom of the world beneath the turning stars, the lessons woven by countless seasons into bone and sinew and sense; they gazed with renewed wonder on the pale Sun and the cold Earth as they awaited the common destiny of all material things.

Therefore the work of this season begins in the quarter of Earth.

Third, face North. While saying the following words, visualize the presence of the elements of Earth and Fire in their quarters, and feel the polarity between them. Say: "North; South. Earth; Fire. The realm of the Body; the realm of the Spirit. May they enter into the great harmony."

Fourth, visualize the presence of the elements of Water and Air in their quarters, and feel the polarity between them. Say: "West; East. Water; Air. The realm of the Heart; the realm of the Mind. May they enter into the great harmony."

Fifth, visualize the presence of all four elements in their quarters, and feel the complex fourfold relationship among them. Say: "The realm of the Stones; the realm of the Winds; the realm of the Flames; the realm of the Waves. May they enter into the great harmony."

Sixth, face East and say: "By the hawk of May in the heights of morning, I invoke the Air and the powers of the Air! May their blessings be with the living Earth during the season to come." While you say this, imagine a blazing star at the zenith, almost infinitely far above the lodge; this is Antares, the Royal Star governing the ceremony.

Seventh, face South and say: "By the white stag of the summer greenwood, I invoke the Fire and the powers of the Fire! May their blessings be with the living Earth during the season to come." While you say this, imagine a ray of light descending from the star at infinite height to the golden sphere of the Sun, blazing at zenith above the lodge, high above but much closer than the star.

Eighth, face West and say: "By the salmon of wisdom who dwells in the sacred pool, I invoke the Water and the powers of the Water! May their blessings be with the living Earth during the season to come." While you say this, imagine the ray of light descending further from the blazing Sun to the sphere of the full Moon standing at the zenith above the lodge, high above but much closer than the Sun.

Ninth, face North and say: "By the great bear who guards the starry heavens, I invoke the Earth and the powers of the Earth! May their blessings be with the living Earth during the season to come." While you say this, imagine the ray of light descending from the shining Moon all the way to the Sphere of Protection you established around the lodge. The entire Sphere is seen to be filled with rainbow-colored light, which radiates outward in all directions.

Tenth, face the altar and say: "In this season of winter may the Sun make manifest the mystery of Light. May the Earth reflect that manifestation in the mystery of Life."

Eleventh, go to the altar and prepare it for the communion ceremony. Then proceed with the communion ceremony as explained earlier in this book.

Twelfth, be seated and enter into meditation, taking the season of winter as your theme. When you have meditated for a time, cast a divination using the Sacred Geometry Oracle or any other divinatory method you prefer, and take it as a guide for your work during the season ahead. Perform the closing ritual to finish.

RESOURCES

Atkinson, William Walker (as Theron Q. Dumont), *The Solar Plexus or Abdominal Brain* (Chicago: Advanced Thought Publishing Co., 1930).
Gardener, Harry J. (as Frater VIII°), *The Golden Gate* (Los Angeles: Golden Dawn Press, 1933).
Gardener, Harry J., *Streamline Minds* (Los Angeles: The Author, 1936).
Gilbert, John, *The Doors of Tarot* (London: Aeon Books, 2023).
Gilbert, John, *The Tree of Spirit* (London: Aeon Books, 2023).
Gray, Henry, *Gray's Anatomy* (New York: Crown, 1978).
Greer, John Michael, *The Ceremony of the Grail* (Woodbury, MN: Llewellyn, 2022).
Greer, John Michael, *The Dolmen Arch* (2 vols.; Portland, OR: Azoth, 2020).
Greer, John Michael, *The Druid Magic Handbook* (York Beach, ME: Weiser, 2007).
Greer, John Michael, *The Fellowship of the Hermetic Rose* (4 vols.; Providence, RI: Creative Commons, 2022).
Greer, John Michael, *The Secret of the Five Rites* (London: Aeon Books, 2024).
Greer, John Michael, *The Secret of the Temple* (Woodbury, MN: Llewellyn, 2020).
Greer, John Michael, *The Way of the Four Elements* (London: Aeon Books, 2024).

Greer, John Michael, *The Way of the Golden Section* (London: Aeon Books, 2021).
Hall, Manly Palmer, *Man, Grand Symbol of the Mysteries* (Los Angeles: Philosophical Research Society, 1972).
Hall, Manly Palmer, *The Occult Anatomy of Man* (Los Angeles: Philosophical Research Society, 1937).
Hall, Manly Palmer, *Self-Unfoldment through Disciplines of Realization* (Los Angeles: Philosophical Research Society, 1946).
Hall, Manly Palmer, *Talks to Students on Occult Philosophy* (Los Angeles: Philosophical Research Society, 1925).
Lévi, Eliphas, *Doctrine and Ritual of High Magic*, Trans. Mark Mikituk and John Michael Greer (New York: Tarcher Perigee, 2017).
Plummer, George Winslow, *Rosicrucian Fundamentals* (New York: Flame Press, 1920).
Plummer, George Winslow, *Rosicrucian Manual* (New York: Mercury, 1923).
Plummer, George Winslow, *Rosicrucian Symbology* (New York: Macoy, 1916).
Plummer, John, *The Many Paths of the Independent Sacramental Movement* (Berkeley, CA: Apocryphile, 2006).
Rele, Vasant G., *The Mysterious Kundalini* (Bombay: D.B. Taraporevala Sons, 1931).
Seton, Julia, *The Psychology of the Solar Plexus and Subconscious Mind* (New York: Edward J. Clode, 1914).
Towne, Elizabeth, *Just How to Wake the Solar Plexus* (Holyoke, MA: The Elizabeth Towne Co., 1907).

INDEX

Note: Page numbers in *italics* indicate figures and references following "n" refer notes.

Abred, 100n16
Acolyte, 73–74. *See also* minor orders
   ceremony of commitment for, 79–81
   training, 77–79
adytum. *See* sanctuary
American occult teachings, xvii–xviii
Ancient Order of Druids in America (AODA), 109, 110
anointing, 64–65
AODA. *See* Ancient Order of Druids in America
Ashley, Juliet, xvi
astral body, 22–23
   strengthening, 48–49
autumn equinox ceremony, 131–133

banishing ritual, 121
baptism sacrament, 41

beginnings, ceremony of new, 41–42
blessing, 59
   and cleansing lodge, 112–114
   mastering art of, 59–60
   with palm centers, 59–60
   sacrament, 59, 76
breathing, 119–120
breathwork, 119–120

cardiac plexuses, 3
Carr-Gomm, Philip, 63
cerebrospinal
   fluid, 5–6
   nervous system, 3
ceremony. *See also* lodge ceremonies
   autumn equinox, 131–133
   Golden Section communion, 96–103
   of new beginnings, 41–42

spring equinox, 127–129
summer solstice, 129–131
winter solstice, 133–135
ceremony of commitment, 44–45
   Acolyte, 75, 77, 79–81
   Cleric, 31–32
   Doorkeeper, 44–45
   Healer, 61, 65–66
   Reader, 55–56
   requirements for, 32
The Ceremony of the Grail (Greer), xix, 14, 109, 110
Ceugant, 100n16
circulation of life force, 86–89
   central spinal channel, 86
   mystics, 87, 88–89, *88*
   occultists, 87–88, *87*
clairflairance, 42–44
clairtangence, 38
Cleric, 25–27. *See also* minor orders
   ceremony of commitment, 31–32
   Divine, 27
   integrating Clerical practices with Doorkeeper training, 40–41
   prayer, 27
   sacrament of blessing, 26, 27–28
   saying grace, 26–27
clerics, 25–26
communion by intinction, 99
Confirmation sacrament, 54
consecration *sub conditione*, xvi

discursive meditation, 118
   balancing tension and relaxation, 119
   breathing, 119–120
   breathwork, 119–120
   Eastern methods of meditation, 118
   Fourfold Breath, 119–120
   meditation, 120–121
   objective mind, 118
   postural awareness in meditation, 119
   posture, 118
   practical guide, 120–121
   relaxation, 119

   setting stage for, 120–121
   theme, 118
   Western path, 118
Divine, xv, 27, 51
divine service sacrament, 76
The Dolmen Arch (Greer), 108–109, 111
Doorkeeper, 39–40. *See also* minor orders
   integrating Clerical practices with Doorkeeper training, 40–41
   path, 53–54
   role of Doorkeeper, 42–44
The Druid Magic Handbook (Greer), 109, 111
ductless glands. *See* endocrine—glands

The Earth Mysteries Workbook (Greer), 108
Eastern methods of meditation, 118
elemental
   symbolism, 74
   working tools, 68
endocrine
   glands, 4
   system, 4–5
energy
   -awakening exercise, 9, 12–14
   clearing, 86–89
   etheric energies, 36
exercise
   energy-awakening, 9, 12–14
   rising call, 9, 11–12
   solar plexus, 9, 10–11
   for stimulating vagus nerve, 9
Exorcist, 60
eye of Dangma. *See* pineal gland
Eye of Revelation. *See* pineal gland

fast food, 26
The Fellowship of the Hermetic Rose (Greer), 109
Fellowship of the Hermetic Rose, 110
festina lente, 18
fifth circle, 57
   anointing and healing prayer, 64–65
   art of listening, 62–63
   blessing with palm centers, 59–60

ceremony of commitment for
    Healer, 65–66
completing, 66
cultivating inner ear of Healer,
    62–63
Exorcist, 60
fifth vortex, 58–59
Healer as Reader, 64
Healer's continued practice and
    growth, 64
healing beyond material, 60–62
healing prayer, 65
hearing and intuition, 62–63
intention and emotion, 64–65
maintaining foundations, 64
mastering art of blessing, 59–60
mental plane and power of
    communication, 58–59
order of Healer, 60–62
sacrament of anointing, 64–65
solar and telluric energies for
    healing, 59–60
spiritual practice of Healer, 60–62
temple design, *58*
temple visualization, 57–58
throat vortex, 58–59
fifth vortex, 58–59. *See also* vortices,
    seven
first circle, 1
    completing, 18
    energy-awakening exercise, 9, 12–14
    exercises for stimulating vagus
        nerve, 9–14
    gnostic lessons, 17–18
    minor orders, 18
    occult anatomy, 1
    rising call exercise, 9, 11–12
    seven vortices, 7–9, *8*
    solar plexus exercise, 9, 10–11
    temple visualization, 14–16
    visualization practice for
        meditation, 14–17
    visualizing guardian angel, 16–17
food, fast, 26
Fortune, Dion, 110
Fourfold Breath, 119–120

fourth circle, 47
    ceremony of commitment
        for Reader, 55–56
    completing, 56
    constructing spiritual foundation,
        47–48
    Doorkeeper's path, 53–54
    fourth vortex, 48–49
    order of Reader, 51–53
    palm centers and two currents,
        49–51
    sacrament of teaching, 54–55
    service and forgiveness, 53–54
    solar and telluric currents, 49–51
    strengthening astral body, 48–49
    temple design, *48*
    temple visualization, 47–48
fourth vortex, 48–49. *See also* vortices,
    seven

Gardener, Harry J., xvii
genital vortex, 36, 59. *See also* vortices,
    seven
"genius", 16n6
Gilbert, John, xiv, xvi, xvii, xviii, 109
gnosis of the universe, xvi
gnosis, xv
gnostics, xiv
    lessons, xvii, 17–18
    priesthood, 76
    teachings, xvi
Golden Rectangle, 20
Golden Section, 20
Golden Section communion ceremony,
    96–97
    altar diagram, *100*
    communion by intinction, 99
    in group workings, 105
    integrating inner and outer
        temples, 105
    requirements of ceremony, 98–99
    ritual setup, 98–99
    steps for performing, 99–103
Golden Section Fellowship, xii, xiii, xix
    autumn equinox ceremony, 131–133
    core training completion, 107

discursive meditation, 118–121
foundations and practices of, 1
Golden Section Fellowship series, 108
initiation ritual for practitioners, 94–96
lodge ceremonies, 121–127
practices, 111
recommended reading, 108–110
resources, 110
seven circles of, xx
Sphere of Protection, 111–117
spring equinox ceremony, 127–129
summer solstice ceremony, 129–131
winter solstice ceremony, 133–135
grace, saying, 26–27
Gray's Anatomy (Gray), 2n5
guardian angel, 16–17
guardian genius. *See* guardian angel
guardian juno. *See* guardian angel
Gwynfydd, 100n16

Hall, Manly Palmer, 2, 110
Healer, 60–62. *See also* minor orders
  anointing and healing prayer, 64–65
  ceremony of commitment for, 65–66
  continued practice and growth, 64
  cultivating inner ear of, 62–63
  Exorcist, 60
  hearing and intuition, 62–63
  maintaining foundations, 64
  as Reader, 64
  sacrament of anointing, 64–65
  spiritual practice of, 60–62
healing. *See also* self-healing
  balancing self and service, 75
  at distance, 94
  legal issues in, 90–91
  with palm centers, 69–70, 89–94
  prayer, 64–65
  solar and telluric energies for, 59–60

holy oil, 32–33
holy order sacrament, 76
holy water, 32–33
human body systems, 2
  cardiac plexuses, 3
  cerebrospinal fluid, 5–6
  cerebrospinal nervous system, 3
  ductless glands/endocrine glands, 4
  endocrine system, 4–5
  hypogastric plexus, 3
  infundibulum, 5
  interstitial fluid, 5
  lymph channels, 5
  pelvic plexus, 3
  pineal gland, 4, 5
  pituitary gland, 4–5
  solar plexus, 3
  sympathetic nervous system, 2–3
  vagus nerve, 2, 6–7
hypogastric plexus, 3

infundibulum, 5
initiate's sphere of protection, 114–117
interstitial fluid, 5
intuition
  and spiritual development, 29–31
  touch and, 77–79

Jesus of Nazareth, xv

knee centers, 22
knee vortices, 22–23. *See also* vortices, seven
Knight, Gareth, 110

Laibow, Rima, xvi
Layton, Bentley, xv
LCC. *See* Liberal Catholic Church
Lesser Banishing Ritual of the Pentagram, 121
Lévi, Eliphas, 2
Liberal Catholic Church (LCC), xv
The Life Force Workbook (Greer), 108
listening, art of, 62–63

lodge ceremonies, 121
    altar diagram, *125*
    closing ceremony, 126–127
    completed opening ritual, *124*
    lodge of Golden Section Fellowship, 121
    opening ceremony, 121–125
    opening ritual, *122*, *123*
    spiritual practice space, 121
    straightedge and compasses, *125*
    Three Rays of Light, 125
lymph channels, 5

marriage sacrament, 76
meditation, 120–121
    Eastern methods of, 118
    postural awareness in, 119
    visualization practice for, 14–17
    Western method of, 118
mental plane and communication, 58–59
mesocosm, 103–104
Michell, John, 110
Middle Pillar, 9
mindful eating, 29–31
minor orders, xvi, 18, 83
    Acolyte, 73–74
    Cleric, 25–27
    Doorkeeper, 39–40
    Healer, 60–62
    Reader, 51–53
    sacraments assigned to, 76
Modern Order of Essenes, 110
Monroe, Robert, xv
mystic senses of the Druid, three, 63

naming sacrament, 41–42, 54, 76
naos. *See* nave
nave, 20–21, 21n9

objective mind, 3, 118
occult anatomy, 1
    hidden dimensions of human body, 1–2
    human body systems, 2–7
    Seen and Unseen, 2
    subjective mind, 2–3
occultism, xii–xiii
    American occult teachings, xvii–xviii
    occult training, xi
    planes of occult tradition, 7
The Occult Philosophy Workbook (Greer), 108

palm centers
    awakening, 23
    awakening left palm, 24
    awakening right palm, 24–25
    blessing with, 59–60
    "bracelet lines", 23
    charging, 36
    charging with element of water, 37–38
    charging with other elements, 38
    development of clairtangence, 38
    drawing triangle and circle, 24–25
    healing others with, 89–94
    healing with, 69–70
    joining centers, 25
    sealing and balancing palm centers, 25
    solar and telluric currents, 25
    and two currents, 49–51
pelvic plexus, 3
personal empowerment ritual, 114–117
pineal center, 13
pineal gland, 4, 5
    and spiritual insight, 68–69
pituitary gland, 4–5, 85
planes of occult tradition, 7
Plummer, George Winslow, xvii
Plummer, John, xv
postural awareness in meditation, 119
posture, 118
prayer, 27
    healing, 65
priesthood, sacraments reserved for, 76
psychic senses, 85–86
psychometry, 79

Reader, 51–53. *See also* minor orders
   ceremony of commitment for, 55–56
   sacrament of teaching, 54–55
relaxation, 119
religion, xiii
rising call exercise, 9, 11–12
ritual
   banishing, 121
   of humble service and vow, 79–81
   personal empowerment, 114–117
   Sphere of Protection, 24, 25, 37, 111, 112–114, 114–117

sacrament, 77
   of anointing, 64–65, 76
   assigned to minor orders, 76
   of baptism, 41
   of blessing, 59, 76
   of Confirmation, 54
   of divine service, 76
   of holy orders, 76
   life as, 76–77
   of marriage, 76
   of naming, 41–42, 54, 76
   reserved for priesthood, 76
   of teaching, 54–55, 76
The Sacred Geometry Oracle (Greer), 108
sacred space, creating, 67–68
sanctuary, 21, 21n9
saying grace, 26–27
science, xiii
second circle, 19
   activating knee vortices, 22–23
   adytum/sanctuary, 21, 21n9
   astral body, 22–23
   awakening palm centers, 23–25
   completing second circle, 33
   enhancing intuition and spiritual development, 29–31
   expanding energy use, 23
   Golden Rectangle, 20
   Golden Section, 20
   holy water and holy oil, 32–33
   knee centers, 22
   mindful eating and nutrition, 29–31
   naos/nave, 20–21, 21n9
   order of Cleric, 25–27, 27–28, 31–32
   seven vortices, 22, 23
   solar plexus, 23
   strengthening connection to material plane, 22–23
   temple design, 19–21, *21*
   temple geometry, *20*
   temple visualization, 19–21
   visualizing turning stars, 22
The Secret of the Five Rites (Greer), xviii, 109
The Secret of the Temple (Greer), xix, 14, 109
secret temple, xix
Seen, 2
self-healing, 89. *See also* healing
   and energetic balance, 89–90
   focused energy healing for imbalances, 72–73
   with palm centers, 69–73
   passes for, 70–72
   working with specific illnesses, 72–73
sense of smell, 42
sensory awareness, 77–79
seventh circle, 83
   building the temple, 103–104
   circulation of life force, 86–89
   communion ceremony, 96–97, 98–103, 105
   completing, 105–106
   enhancing psychic senses, 85–86
   form of initiation, 94
   healing others with palm centers, 89–94
   initiation ritual, 94–96
   mesocosm, 103–104
   path to priesthood, 83–84
   self-healing and energetic balance, 89–90
   seventh vortex, 85–86
   spiritual growth and energy clearing, 86–89
   temple as mesocosm, 103–104
   temple visualization, 84–85

seventh vortex, 85–86. *See also* vortices, seven
seven vortices. *See* vortices, seven
Shaw, Matthew, xiv, xvi, xvii, xviii
sixth circle, 67
    Acolyte training, 77–79
    awakening soul and integrating self, 73–74
    balancing self and service, 75
    ceremony of commitment for Acolyte, 79–81
    completing, 81
    creating sacred space, 67–68
    developing sensory awareness, 77–79
    elemental working tools, 68
    expanding Healer's path, 75
    healing with palm centers, 69–70
    life as sacrament, 76–77
    order of Acolyte, 73–74
    pineal gland and spiritual insight, 68–69
    ritual of humble service and vow, 79–81
    ritual understanding, 77–79
    self-healing with palm centers, 69–73
    sixth vortex, 68–69
    spiritual path of everyday actions, 76–77
    temple design, *68*
    temple visualization, 67–68
    touch and intuition, 77–79
sixth vortex, 68–69. *See also* vortices, seven
smell, 42–44
Smith, Warren, xvi
Societas Rosicruciana in America (SRIA), xvii
solar current, 49–51, 59–60, 97
solar plexus, 3, 23
    exercise, 9, 10–11
Sphere of Protection, 111
    blessing and cleansing lodge, 112–114
    individual version, 114–117

    initiate's sphere of protection, 114–117
    lodge version, 112–114
    personal empowerment ritual, 114–117
    ritual, 24, 25, 37, 111, 112–114, 114–117
spiritual
    foundation, 47–48
    growth, 86–89
    guardian. *See* guardian angel
    practice space, 121
Spiritual Alchemy, Order of, 110
spiritual energy work, 91
    ethics and legal considerations, 90–91
    healing at distance, 94
    method of working, 92–93
    methods and ethics of distance, 94
    techniques for conducting session, 92–93
spring equinox ceremony, 127–129
SRIA. *See* Societas Rosicruciana in America
Stubblebine, Albert, xvi
subjective mind, 2–3
summer solstice ceremony, 129–131
sutala chakras. *See* knee centers
Symanski, Owen, xiv, xvi
sympathetic nervous system, 2–3

teaching sacrament, 54–55, 76
telluric current, 49–51, 59–60, 97
temple
    design, 19–21, *21*, *48*, *58*, *68*
    geometry, *20*
    integrating inner and outer, 105
    as mesocosm, 103–104
    secret temple, xix
    tradition, xviii–xix
temple visualization, 19
    phase one, 14–16
    phase two, 19–21
    phase three, 35–36
    phase four, 47–48
    phase five, 57–58

phase six, 67–68
phase seven, 84–85
tension and relaxation, 119
theme, 118
third circle, 35
    activating genital vortex, 36
    awakening clairflairance, 42–44
    balancing etheric energies, 36
    ceremony of commitment, 44–45
    ceremony of new beginnings, 41–42
    charging palm centers, 36–38
    completing third circle, 45
    emotional mastery and spiritual growth, 39–40
    integrating Clerical practices with Doorkeeper training, 40–41
    order of Doorkeeper, 39–40
    psychic sense of smell, 42–44
    role of Doorkeeper, 42–44
    sacrament of naming, 41–42
    smell and intuition, 42–44
    temple visualization, 35–36
    third vortex, 36
"third eye". *See* pituitary gland
third vortex, 36. *See also* vortices, seven
Three Rays of Light, 125
throat vortex, 58–59. *See also* vortices, seven
touch and intuition, 77–79
turning stars, visualizing, 22

universal gnosis, xvi
Universal Gnostic Church (UGC), xiv, 25, 110
    Acolyte, 79–81
    bishops, xiv, xvi
    Cleric, 25–27, 31–32
    consecration *sub conditione*, xvi
    Divine, xv
    Doorkeeper, 39–40, 44–45
    gnosis of the universe, xvi
    Gnostic Lessons, xvii
    Healer, 60–62, 65–66
    minor orders, xvi, 18, 83
    priesthood of, xvi–xvii
    Reader, 51–53
    sacraments assigned to minor orders, 76
    Shaw, Matthew, xiv, xvi, xvii
    Symanski, Owen, xiv, xvi
    universal gnosis, xvi
    Zasluchy, Omar, xiv, xvi
Unseen, 2

vagus nerve, 2, 6–7, 119
    exercises for stimulating, 9
visualization practice for meditation, 14–17
vortices, seven, 7–9, *8*, 22, 23
    fifth vortex, 58–59
    fourth vortex, 48–49
    genital vortex, 36, 59
    knee vortices, 22–23
    seventh vortex, 85–86
    sixth vortex, 9, 68–69
    third vortex, 36
    throat vortex, 58–59

The Way of the Four Elements (Greer), xi, xii, 37, 38, 97, 105, 107, 108, 111
The Way of the Golden Section (Greer), xi, xii, 1, 3, 107, 108, 111
Western occultism, xiv, 118
    American occult teachings, vii–xviii
    sources of teachings, xiv–xix
    temple tradition, xviii–xix
    Universal Gnostic Church, xiv–xvii
winter solstice ceremony, 133–135

Zasluchy, Omar, xiv, xvi

www.ingramcontent.com/pod-product-compliance
Ingram Content Group UK Ltd.
Pitfield, Milton Keynes, MK11 3LW, UK
UKHW021825280425
457948UK00017B/199